Amphibians
&Reptiles of
Yellowstone and
Grand Teton
National Parks

Amphibians & Reptiles of Yellowstone and Grand Teton National Parks

Edward D. Koch

Charles R. Peterson

UNIVERSITY OF UTAH PRESS
Salt Lake City

Published with assistance from The Yellowstone Association

Cover photographs: FRONT, boreal chorus frog; BACK, garter snake

LIBRARY OF CONGRESS CATALOGING IN PUBLICATION DATA

Koch, Edward D., 1963–
    Amphibians & reptiles of Yellowstone and Grand Teton national
parks / Edward D. Koch, Charles R. Peterson.
        p.   cm.
    Includes bibliographical references (p.   ) and index.
    ISBN 0-87480-472-8
    1. Amphibians—Yellowstone National Park.   2. Reptiles—
Yellowstone National Park.   3. Amphibians—Wyoming—Grand Teton
National Park.   4. Reptiles—Wyoming—Grand Teton National Park.
5. Yellowstone National Park.   6. Grand Teton National Park (Wyo.)
I. Peterson, Charles, 1949—   .   II. Title.
QL653.Y44K63   1995
597.6'09787'5—dc20   95-24058

We dedicate this book to Dr. Frederick B. Turner and Dr. Charles C. Carpenter, who pioneered the study of amphibians and reptiles in Yellowstone and Grand Teton National Parks forty years ago and who helped greatly in preparation of this book.

Contents

Foreword

WE BEGAN WORKING together to gather the information that eventually formed the basis of this book because of our common interest in amphibians and reptiles and because we lived and worked in and around the Greater Yellowstone Ecosystem. The book actually had its beginning in 1988 as a class project for a herpetology (study of amphibians and reptiles) course at Idaho State University. The goal of the project was to analyze the distribution of amphibians and reptiles in Yellowstone National Park (hereafter referred to simply as "Yellowstone"). We soon discovered, however, that because so little information existed concerning the herpetofauna (amphibian and reptile species) of Yellowstone, we would first have to determine where these animals occurred before we could study the factors influencing their distribution.

So, for the past six years, we have been gathering information on the herpetofauna of this park. John Varley, then chief of research for Yellowstone, encouraged us in this endeavor and suggested that we prepare a guide to the amphibians and reptiles of Yellowstone and of Grand Teton National Park (hereafter referred to simply as "the Tetons"). Our initial efforts focused only on Yellowstone's herpetofauna, but in 1991 we began collecting data in the Tetons to try and provide a more comprehensive book with a wider appeal. Because we have spent less time in the Tetons than we have in Yellowstone, however, we have less information for that park.

We have three primary goals for this book. First, we hope to provide information for individuals to identify the region's amphibians and reptiles. Second, we want to summarize and share what we have learned about these interesting and ecologically important but generally unappreciated animals. In writing this book, we have tried to combine a readable style with careful documentation of information sources typical of a scientific paper.

Third, we hope that the existence of this book will stimulate interest in the amphibians and reptiles of these two magnificent parks so that future publications can be more comprehensive and detailed, filling in many information gaps that still exist today. This book should be looked upon as a call to action for all those interested in the region's amphibians and reptiles to make and record observations to improve our collective understanding (see chapter entitled "Information Needs: How You Can Contribute").

As you will see, much remains to be learned about the region's amphibians and reptiles.

Acknowledgments

MANY INDIVIDUALS AND organizations helped with this project, and we are grateful to all of them. First we thank the Yellowstone Association for their generous financial assistance in publishing this book. Thanks also to John Varley and Stu Coleman of Yellowstone National Park for their support and encouragement in preparing this book. Paul Schullery's guidance during the final stages of preparation of the manuscript was excellent. Pete Hayden and the staff at the Grand Teton National Park helped greatly in familiarizing us with the park and its amphibians and reptiles so that we could broaden the scope of this book.

The U.S. Fish and Wildlife Service Fisheries Assistance Office in Yellowstone provided us with the Backcountry Lakes Survey Data and logistical support. The Old Faithful Subdistrict Ranger staff and naturalist staff assisted us in several ways. The Department of Biological Sciences at Idaho State University and the Idaho Museum of Natural History also supported this project in a variety of ways. We thank all of the museum personnel throughout the country who provided us with information on museum specimens in their care.

Many people provided us with multiple observations of amphibians and reptiles and information on their habitats, including: Roger Andrasik, Mary Beth Baptiste, Sara Broadbent, Denise Culver, Katy Duffy, Gregg Fauth, Chris and Susan Glenn, Dale Gomez, Paul Greguoli, Steve Hill, Rick Hutchinson, Nancy Kehoe, Kristen Legg, Craig McClure, Pat Motheney, Tom Oliff, Dan Reinhart, Carolyn Smithee, Sandy Snell, Eric Stone, Polly Thornton, Jeanine Wagner, Jennifer Whipple, and Richard and Nadia Seigel. Yellowstone National Park naturalist Roy Wood enthusiastically participated in making observations and substantially improved the quality of the distribution maps for several species in this book as well as our knowledge of the life history aspects of Yellowstone's amphibians and reptiles.

We thank Dr. Fred Turner, University of California, Los Angeles, and Dr. Charles Carpenter, University of Oklahoma, for their willingness to share their considerable knowledge about the amphibians and reptiles of Yellowstone and the Tetons, respectively. We also appreciate their help in reviewing the draft text to ensure accuracy while improving "readability" of the book. Dr. George Baxter, when reviewing the rough draft, provided thoughtful comments and suggestions as well as some of his personal observations of these animals. Paul Bartelt, Ray Clark, Vince Cobb, Mike Dorcas, and Debra Patla also reviewed accounts for those species on which they have expertise.

Steven Hill of Montana State University supplied a great deal of preliminary data from his research on tiger salamanders at Ice Lake Reservoir near Gardiner, Montana, in Yellowstone; preliminary data from other research projects; and helpful comments on the draft manuscript. Lee Whittlesey reviewed a draft of the book with an eye toward ensuring accuracy of any historical information. He also shared with us some additional historical information of which we were previously unaware. Bill Leonard, Dr. Robert Moore, Marjorie L. Peterson, Dave Ross, and Bruce Zoellick also reviewed the text to ensure that thoughts were communicated with clarity. Jeffrey Grathwohl and others at the University of Utah Press were very helpful in finalizing many aspects of the book.

Chris Askey, Paul Bartelt, Christine Britton, Ray Clark, Stephen Corn, Mike Dorcas, Debra Patla, and Stephen Sullivan helped with fieldwork. We especially thank Paul Bartelt for his efforts in preparing the distribution maps. George McKay, Geographic Information System specialist for the National Park Service, and Jonathan Beck and Ray Clark from Idaho State University also helped prepare the maps. Thanks also to Environmental Science Research, Inc. (ESRI) for assistance with their PC-ARC/INFO Geographic Information System computer program, which was used to generate the distribution maps.

Laureen, Shane, and Kaileen Koch were wonderfully patient and supportive throughout this project. Finally, we thank everyone else who provided us with many valuable observations of Yellowstone and Grand Teton National Parks' amphibians and reptiles.

Edward D. Koch
Charles R. Peterson

How to Use This Book

IN ADDITION TO indicating general headings, the "Contents" section also serves as a checklist of the amphibians and reptiles in the parks. The introduction provides background information on Yellowstone and Grand Teton National Parks and the amphibian and reptile species that occur there. Use the simplified key to identify juvenile or adult amphibians and reptiles.

At the beginning of the species accounts, general descriptions of amphibians or reptiles are presented for each of these two classes of animals. Following the general descriptions are the individual species accounts. Each account has color photographs of that species, and photographs of habitats where that species was found. Almost all the photographs depict animals from the region covered by this book. Each picture caption identifies the locality where the animal was seen or collected.

A dot distribution map is also provided for each species. Refer to the base map on page 3 for reference points for each dot distribution map. A separate chapter, "Other Reported or Potential Species," discusses species that may occur in one or both of the parks or that have been reported but cannot yet be considered confirmed because they have been so infrequently encountered.

The chapter "Information Needs: How You Can Contribute" encourages you to report your amphibian and reptile observations to park personnel. It provides examples of the kinds of information that will be especially useful and a sample data form.

Following the text, there are four aids to the reader: The "References Cited" lists the sources of much of the information in the book. The "Additional References" lists other information sources from the region that are not cited in the text. The "Glossary" explains unfamiliar terms. The "Index" will help you search for key words, headings, or concepts in the text. Finally, if you're wondering just what kind of people would take on a project like this, there is a brief description of us.

We have intentionally repeated ourselves many times throughout the book so the book does not have to be read sequentially in order for the reader to understand points being made.

Reading the following questions and answers should help you to better understand and use this book.

How do I find a particular species description?

There are only 12 species of amphibians and reptiles that we know occur in Yellowstone and Grand Teton National Parks. Therefore, unlike using a guide to plants or birds, finding a particular species account in this book is easy: Just look at the brief list of species in the table of contents. If you are unsure how to identify a particular amphibian or reptile in which you are interested, refer to the simplified key.

What is the key used for?

The simplified key is a means for identifying the juvenile and adult forms of the amphibians and reptiles of Yellowstone and the Tetons. The key describes the characteristics distinguishing one species of amphibian or reptile from another. Instructions on how to use the key are given in the text at the beginning of that chapter.

What do some of the features in the text mean?

We use the standard scientific convention for listing publications in the References Cited section. For example, if a citation in the text reads "(Turner 1955)" or "Turner (1955)," turn to the references and look for the author's name – Turner, F. B. – and the date following the name – 1955. That is the publication we used to supply the particular piece of information associated with the reference. Statements followed by a person's name and then "personal communication" mean that the person so named provided us with the information either verbally or by letter. Statements followed by a person's name and "unpublished data" mean that the person so named actually has data on the matter, but the data have not been made available in published format. If a statement is not followed by a citation, that information is based on our experience (which we generally try to specify) or is assumed to be common knowledge among herpetologists (scientists who study amphibians and reptiles). By including the "Additional References" (which were not cited in the text) we have attempted to list all specific references to amphibians and reptiles in this region of which we are aware.

How do I use the common and scientific names?

We use standard references to scientific names in the species accounts. For example, the "generic" name (that is, the name of the genus) of the blotched tiger salamander is *Ambystoma;* the "specific" name (that is, the name distinguishing the species) is *tigrinum,* and the subspecific name is *melanostictum.* The two garter snake species in this book are closely related enough to be included in the same genus and, not coincidentally, are perhaps the most difficult species in the parks to distinguish from each other. The scientific name for the valley garter snake is *Thamnophis sirtalis fitchi* and for the wandering garter snake is *Thamnophis elegans vagrans.*

Why does the common name of a species sometimes differ in this book?

For eight of the twelve types of amphibians and reptiles covered in this book, there are common names for both the species and the subspecies found in this region. For example, the rattlesnake found in Yellowstone National Park could correctly be referred to as the western rattlesnake *(Crotalus viridis)* or the prairie rattlesnake *(Crotalus viridis viridis).* Most often, we refer to the common name for the subspecies as it is listed in the table of contents (except for the spotted frog, northern leopard frog, bullfrog, and rubber boa, which have no subspecific designation). When we wish to include information for other subspecies, we use the common name for the species. There are also numerous instances where, for the sake of the reader, we try to avoid continuously repeating the entire common name if it is not specifically necessary to do so (for example, salamander, or tiger salamander, instead of blotched tiger salamander). For common names, we referred to Collins (1990).

How are some of the place names used?

We often use the simpler terms: "Yellowstone" to refer to Yellowstone National Park and "the Tetons" to refer to Grand Teton National Park. Jackson Hole is the valley, or "hole," which today lies mostly within Grand Teton National Park, but previous to 1950 it was not formally part of the park. We sometimes refer to this specific portion of the Tetons as Jackson Hole, and we always do so if the subject of the discussion predates 1950. The term "Teton Mountain Range" refers to exactly that—the range of mountains within Grand Teton National Park. We also use the term "Greater Yellowstone Ecosystem," now commonly accepted, to refer to the area in and around both national parks.

What are the units of measure used?

The units of measure we use in this book are metric (with nonmetric equivalents in parentheses). The following is a list of the two types (abbreviated).

Metric	Nonmetric
1 cm (centimeter)	= 0.39 in. (inch)
1 m (meter)	= 3.28 ft (feet)
1 km (kilometer)	= 0.58 mi (miles)
1 g (gram)	= 0.04 oz (ounce)

Conversion of temperature units requires the use of a mathematical equation, but in general, a change of one degree celsius (°C) equals a change of 1.8 degrees Fahrenheit (°F). To convert a number from degrees Celsius to degrees Fahrenheit, multiply the number by ⁹⁄₅ and then add 32. To convert from Fahrenheit to Celsius, subtract 32 and then multiply by ⁵⁄₉.

How do I use the maps?

The distribution maps describe only those sites where individuals of a species have been collected or carefully observed and documented. The red dots indicate museum collection records, which are specimens that have been collected and preserved in a museum as a permanent record and for future researchers to study. Note that collecting animals in the parks without a permit is *not* allowed. The green dots indicate observations for which no specimens were collected but that we consider reliable. Most of the symbols on the maps are green dots because most of the data we used for developing the maps were observations of animals that were left where they were found. Uncertain observations that may represent a range extension or are otherwise noteworthy are indicated by question marks on the maps.

We think that most of the distribution maps are incomplete. This statement is especially true for areas away from roads. Just because a symbol does not appear on a particular part of a species map, do not automatically conclude that the species does not occur there. You should also read the text describing the distribution of that species. Many observations are important to share, especially for areas in which the species has not been previously recorded, so please take the time to carefully report such observations to park authorities (see chapter entitled "Information Needs: How You Can Contribute"). Other map features include the park borders, roads, rivers, lakes, and the continental divide.

Several steps were involved in generating the distribution maps for each species. The base map was developed by digitizing some features of the U.S. Geological Survey maps for each park, using the SigmaScan computer program (Jandel Scientific, Inc., San Rafael, California). The scale of the Yellowstone map was 1:125,000, and scale of the Teton map was 1:62,500. Locations of animal occurrence records were then digitized off of these same maps. The accuracy of each occurrence record depended on the detail of the description of the location. The coordinates of some locations could be identified quite accurately (for example, within 100 m [333 ft]). The accuracy of some records was much lower because of the size of the geographic features with which they were associated. For example, if a rubber boa was described as being observed in Bechler Canyon, we could only locate it to within about 3 km (1.86 mi). We were unable to plot the locations of some records because they could not be closely associated with a known geographic feature (body of water, road, thermal feature, trail, and so on). The ARC-INFO computer program (ESRI, Redlands, California) was then used to combine data sets and generate the maps. Most of the mapping work was done by Paul Bartelt, a Ph.D. candidate at Idaho State University.

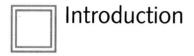 Introduction

The Physical Environment of the Region

THE AREA KNOWN AS Yellowstone National Park has been referred to as "the crown jewel of America's national parks," the best of the best. It also is this nation's first national park, having been established in 1872. Grand Teton National Park was established in 1929, encompassing an area much smaller than today's park. The Jackson National Monument in the Jackson Hole valley was created in 1943 and was incorporated into the national park in 1950. This park now includes the impressive Teton Mountain Range and one of the most scenic mountain valleys in the world, Jackson Hole. Yellowstone and Grand Teton National Parks make up a special place, protected in perpetuity by law, "for the benefit and enjoyment of the people." The parks are available for all to enjoy, for conservation of natural resources, recreational use, aesthetic appreciation, and scientific study.

Together, Yellowstone National Park (or just "Yellowstone") and Grand Teton National Park (or just "the Tetons") form the core (about one quarter) of an area that is often referred to as the Greater Yellowstone Ecosystem (Keiter and Boyce 1991). This area is believed by many to be the largest, essentially intact ecosystem in the temperate zones of the earth. It still harbors almost all its native flora and fauna, including the popular large mammals such

1

The region is famous in part for its assemblage of large mammals. Bison (or "buffalo") such as this animal in Hayden Valley in Yellowstone frequently cause traffic jams along park roads from visitors stopping to observe them.

as grizzly bears and bison. Both Yellowstone and the Tetons are characterized by rugged and remote country with harsh weather conditions. It is a land where natural forces such as wind, water, erosion, fire, and even volcanic activity still shape the environment as they have for thousands of years. Even today many aspects of this region remain unknown. This lack of knowledge seems especially true of the amphibians and reptiles that live there.

Yellowstone encompasses about 8992 km² (3472 mi², or 2.2 million acres) of land. The Tetons encompass 1222 km² (472 mi², or 300,000 acres). Elevations within both parks range from about 1609 m (5280 ft) where the Yellowstone River leaves Yellowstone National Park in the north on its way to the Atlantic Ocean, to over 4200 m (nearly 13,800 ft) at the peak of the Grand Teton. Yellowstone Lake is the largest lake in North America at such a high elevation—2357 m (7733 ft)—and Shoshone Lake is the largest backcountry lake in the lower 48 states. The Snake River

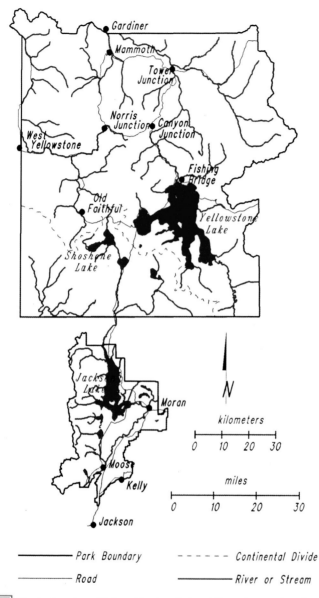

The Yellowstone National Park and Grand Teton National Park region. Park borders are in black, as are park roads. Water bodies are in blue, with the major lakes labeled. The Yellowstone River flows through Yellowstone Lake and exits Yellowstone Park to the north near Gardiner, Montana; the Snake River flows out of Yellowstone south through the Tetons; the Falls and Bechler Rivers join and exit Yellowstone in the southwest corner, the Madison flows out through West Yellowstone, the Gallatin River flows out of Yellowstone's northwest corner, and the Shoshone River exits Yellowstone to the east.

Spectacular mountain scenery, such as this view of the Teton Range from the oxbow along the Snake River draws visitors from around the world to Grand Teton National Park. All species known to occur in this park could be found here, except for the leopard frog, bullfrog, and sagebrush lizard.

in Grand Teton National Park is a large, high-elevation Rocky Mountain river that flows through Jackson Hole past the rugged Teton Mountain Range on its way to the Pacific Ocean. It passes through Jackson Lake, which has been increased over its original size by water impounded behind a dam near the outlet of the natural lake. The Greater Yellowstone Ecosystem also harbors the highest concentration of geothermal features in the world, including more than 60% of all known geysers on the planet (Bryan 1986). These geothermal features and the steep mountain faces of the Tetons are clues to some of the cataclysmic geologic events of the region's past, which have helped make this region so special and have influenced its herpetofauna.

The formation of Yellowstone Lake, the Yellowstone Plateau, the Teton Mountain Range, and the magnificent geothermal features found throughout the region are a result of dynamic and still active geological processes. Six hundred thousand years ago a mountain stood in what is now Yellowstone Lake. At that time, a

Yellowstone's geothermal features helped prompt Congress to protect the region as the world's first national park. Sagebrush lizards occur in the surrounding hills near this small geyser in the Shoshone Geyser Basin on the western shore of Shoshone Lake.

gigantic explosion blew the top of the mountain into the sky, creating an ash cloud that probably persisted for a long time, and wiped out most vertebrate animals (including any amphibians and reptiles) in the area. A caldera, or crater, subsequently formed, and part of it helped form Yellowstone Lake (Pierce 1987). All this volcanic activity occurred only an instant ago in geologic time, and the heat of the earth's core is still very close to the surface in Yellowstone country. This heat is the energy that drives Yellowstone's famous thermal features. Movement of the earth's crust is still occurring today; nearly 2,000 small "earthquakes" occur here each year, which are imperceptible to people but measurable by sensitive scientific equipment (Bryan 1986).

The Teton Mountain Range lies along an active fault line, where one portion of the earth's crust has been rising over the adjacent portion for the last 8 to 10 million years (Clark 1981). In some areas along this fault line, the difference in vertical displacement of the earth's crust approaches 9000 m (30,000 ft)! The activity along this fault line is what thrust the earth skyward and formed the Teton Mountain Range, which is one of the younger mountain ranges in the world. Recent glacial activity and erosion from wind and water have helped to fill the valley floor with rocks and dirt. Today the difference in elevation between the flat valley floor of Jackson Hole and the mountain peaks is about 2100 m (7000 ft). Glacial activity has not only heavily altered the landscape but has probably had a significant influence on the distribution and species occurrence of amphibians and reptiles here. Temporary displacement of animals probably occurred as glaciers advanced and retreated, forcing them to recolonize parts of the region from adjacent areas.

The continental divide runs through Yellowstone National Park, and just to the east of Grand Teton National Park. Water that lands on the east side of the divide runs to the Atlantic Ocean, and water that lands on the west side of the divide runs to the Pacific Ocean. Confusion reigns, though, on Two-Ocean Plateau, east of the Tetons and south of Yellowstone. As the name implies, water resting on this plateau could end up flowing in either of two directions. If it makes its way east, it ends up in Atlantic Creek. If it makes its way west, it flows down Pacific Creek.

The two parks also harbor the headwaters of two major North American river systems. The Snake River and the Falls River eventually join in Idaho and meet the Columbia River in the state of Washington; the Yellowstone, Madison, Gallatin, and Shoshone Rivers run into the Missouri River, which eventually joins the Mississippi River in the state of Missouri. The headwaters of the Green River, which eventually flow into the Colorado River, also occur in the Greater Yellowstone Ecosystem just southeast of the border of Grand Teton National Park. The fact that the continental divide bisects this region influences which subspecies of amphibians and reptiles occur at a particular location.

Vegetation found in this portion of the Rocky Mountains generally consists of coniferous forests (pine, spruce, or fir trees) and, at lower elevations, sagebrush grasslands. These vegetation types indicate the region's cold, snowy winters and dry summers. The plant communities found in this Rocky Mountain ecosystem depend in many ways on fire, and fire is an important process in the ecosystem. For example, some cones of the lodgepole pine will only release their seeds when exposed to heat such as that from a fire. Many other species of wildlife depend on areas that have been recently burned for some of their needs, such as bird species depending on nesting cavities in dead trees, or the region's large mammals depending on meadow grasses for forage. Climate and vegetation, in turn, may affect the presence of amphibians and reptiles.

Past Efforts to Study Amphibians and Reptiles in the Region

When we began our research on the region's amphibians and reptiles in 1988, we learned that little information was available on these animals in Yellowstone and the Tetons. New, basic information can be discovered even more than a century after the region was first studied by people of European heritage. For example, the rubber boa was not documented as occurring in Yellowstone until Herma Albertson (1928) found a specimen in the Old Faithful area in 1928. We now know that the valley garter snake (a subspecies of the common garter snake, which is perhaps the commonest reptile species in all of North America) occurs in limited areas of Yellowstone National Park, although it was never collected in Yellowstone by scientists until 1978. And in 1992 we confirmed that the northern sagebrush lizard occurs in Grand Teton National Park. The next closest area where this species was previously known to occur is over 100 km (60 mi) away. These discoveries occurred from 30 to more than 100 years after these areas gained fame as national parks. The fact is that few people have ever attempted to describe the distribution and abundance of amphibians and reptiles in Yellowstone or the Tetons. New discoveries are waiting for the curious visitor to observe and report (see chapter "Information Needs: How You Can Contribute").

Among those who surveyed amphibians and reptiles in the past are Dorr C. Yeager (1929) and Frederick B. Turner (1951, 1955) in Yellowstone, and Charles C. Carpenter (1953a) in Jackson Hole. Yeager (1929) described the distribution of reptiles in Yellowstone, with notes on amphibians. Much of the information and speculation Yeager provided appears to be true today. However,

In addition to his assessment of amphibians and reptiles of Yellowstone in 1955, pioneering herpetologist Fred Turner completed what today remains among the most detailed natural history studies of the spotted frog. In this 1950s photograph Turner records the call of the spotted frog along Lodge Creek on the northeast shore of Yellowstone Lake where we continue to monitor amphibian populations today.

Another pioneering herpetologist for the Tetons, Chuck Carpenter (left) conducted thorough surveys of the herpetofauna of the Jackson Hole region in the 1950s. His work has enabled us to make valuable comparisons to what we observe today.

both Turner (1951) and we question the likelihood of turtles existing in the park (see chapter entitled "Other Reported or Potential
Species").

Turner (1951) compiled a checklist and prepared a guide (1955)
to the amphibians and reptiles of Yellowstone. These projects
were completed during his tenure as a ranger naturalist and while
he conducted his doctoral thesis research on spotted frogs on
Lodge (Soldier) Creek near the Yellowstone Lake Lodge (see his
publications cited in the references sections). We found Turner's
efforts to describe the amphibians and reptiles of Yellowstone to
be quite accurate. In addition, his detailed studies of the spotted
frog remain among the best ever completed.

Charles Carpenter (1953a) published a scientific paper on the
herpetofauna of Jackson Hole, and additional notes on specific
subjects. He primarily surveyed along the Snake River in the Jackson Hole valley and along Jackson Lake. He also ventured to Togwotee Pass east of Jackson Hole and made many interesting observations at higher-elevation sites.

Charles Mueller (1967) and George Algard (1968) studied the
thermal biology and distribution of the northern sagebrush lizard
in Yellowstone in the mid-1960s while they were graduate stu-
dents at Montana State University. Their studies are still the only
ones focusing on the unique distribution and use of thermal resources for this species in Yellowstone.

Recently we initiated a long-term amphibian population monitoring program in the region (Peterson et al. 1992). We began by
selecting eight sites representing a variety of locations and habitat
types. Generally, these are areas where amphibians have been
known to occur historically and where they still occur today. With
support from the National Park Service, we have visited these
sites regularly since 1991 to monitor the presence and relative
abundance of each species of amphibian present. These data could
be important for evaluating long-term population trends (see section on declining amphibian populations in this chapter). We have
concluded so far that boreal toads appear to be less abundant today
than they were historically, and that leopard frogs appear to be
extinct in this region.

In evaluating all historical information on amphibians and reptiles in the two parks, we found only three data sets providing some degree of information on population sizes. These sets include Fred Turner's spotted frog data, Chuck Carpenter's boreal toad data, and George Algard's northern sagebrush lizard data. Unfortunately, in the 30 to 40 years since the completion of these studies, all three study sites have been radically and irreversibly altered by human activities such as dam construction and river channelization, water development, and road and building development. This development has negated these excellent and rare opportunities to make comparisons within populations over long periods of time. However, resource managers in the parks today are beginning to recognize the need to avoid these kinds of disturbances.

With the additional data available today, we are able to build on the initial works of these pioneer herpetologists and expand our knowledge of the distribution, abundance, and life-history aspects of Yellowstone's and the Tetons' amphibians and reptiles. However, as you will find, much remains to be learned.

The Preparation of This Book

This book extends the work of previous authors by covering both parks, by adding many new observations, by providing distribution maps and color photographs, and by incorporating the now much larger body of scientific information available to us on these animals from throughout their ranges. We attempt to summarize what we have learned from reviewing pertinent literature, contacting over one hundred national and regional museums, reviewing park observation records, soliciting observations from park personnel and visitors, from collaborating with others, and from our own field observations.

At the beginning of our research in 1988, we focused primarily on Yellowstone National Park. At that time only 350 specimen records were known to exist for 9 of the 10 species known to occur in Yellowstone (we had not yet rigorously documented the valley garter snake in Yellowstone) (Koch and Peterson 1989). Of these 350 records, nearly all recorded sites were adjacent to roads and over 60% were for the spotted frog alone. In 1991 we had approximately 200 records for Grand Teton National Park, virtually all of which were in the Jackson Hole valley. Since then we have increased the number of records in both parks combined to nearly 1,000 — most of them observations — including several more records in backcountry areas. Even so, the relative scarcity of data and the inconsistent manner in which they were collected do not allow us to describe comprehensively the distribution of many of the species, although several inferences and generalizations can be made.

We must point out that our knowledge of the amphibians and reptiles of Grand Teton National Park is not as great as that for Yellowstone National Park because we have spent more time in Yellowstone. Even in Yellowstone, we have not had the opportunity to follow up many leads concerning range extensions of species known to occur within the park, or even the possible occurrence of species new to the park. It is our sincere hope that, with publication of this book and an increased awareness of amphibians and reptiles, much can be added to the present knowledge of these animals in Yellowstone and the Tetons.

Present Status of Amphibians and Reptiles

We believe that four species of amphibians and six species of reptiles occur now in Yellowstone National Park. In Grand Teton National Park six species of amphibians and only four species of reptiles are known to occur or have occurred in the recent past. This number of species in both parks (12 overall) is low compared to other areas in the United States (Kiester 1971). This low number presumably is due to the recent disturbance from glacial activity and the cool, dry climate inhibiting colonization by animals less tolerant of such conditions. Only "generalist" species, or species that can tolerate a wide range of living conditions, survive here. All species of amphibians and reptiles found in the parks are widely distributed throughout much of the western United States, and, for some, throughout much of North America.

The distributions of each species of amphibian and reptile within the two parks vary. Blotched tiger salamanders, boreal toads, boreal chorus frogs, spotted frogs, and wandering garter snakes appear to be widely distributed within both parks. Although occurrence records for rubber boas do not indicate a wide distribution, we believe that future sampling will show this species is also widespread. Two species have limited distributions within Yellowstone; the bull snake and the prairie rattlesnake appear to be limited to the northern portion of Yellowstone where the Yellowstone River crosses the park boundary. Existence of the gopher snake (which is the same species as, but a different subspecies than the bull snake) has been reported west of the continental divide in the Tetons, but it has not yet been confirmed here. We suspect that rattlesnakes probably do not occur in the Tetons.

The northern sagebrush lizard may have the most intriguing distribution of all. This species occurs along the last few miles of the Yellowstone River before it leaves Yellowstone Park, and it is also found in isolated, geothermally active areas at higher elevations. Recently, we confirmed the existence of the northern sagebrush lizard at a comparatively high-elevation site in the Tetons that does not appear to be geothermally influenced. It also has been reported elsewhere in the region but the reports have yet to be confirmed. The valley garter snake occurs in the Tetons and the southwest corner of Yellowstone but appears to have declined in abundance. Forty years ago the northern leopard frog was collected at three sites in the Tetons (String, Jenny, and Beaver Dick Lakes), but recent efforts to find this species have been unsuccessful. The bullfrog was introduced to Kelly Warm Springs in Jackson Hole and still occurs there. We believe no turtles occur naturally in either national park.

Vegetative Communities and General Habitat Associations

In Yellowstone and Grand Teton National parks, a wide variety of habitat types are represented. They range from hot, arid, desertlike conditions with sagebrush grasslands and prickly pear cactus near Yellowstone's north entrance, up through several forest habitat types to alpine tundralike conditions at high altitudes in both parks. Knight and Wallace (1989) identified eight separate characteristic vegetative patterns in Yellowstone:

Forested types:
    Lodgepole pine (the most dominant forest type)
    Englemann spruce and subalpine fir
    Douglas fir
    Aspen
    Limber pine and whitebark pine
Nonforested types:
    Sagebrush grasslands
    Mountain meadows
    Sedge/grass and willow riparian

Clark (1981) identified all vegetation patterns listed above as occurring in Jackson Hole (he did not list separately the limber pine/whitebark pine community, although it does occur here) plus an additional three "biotic communities":

Forested type:
    Juniper
Nonforested types:
    Aquatic
    Alpine tundra

Throughout both parks, key habitat associations for all but three species discussed in this book (the northern sagebrush lizard, bull snake, and prairie rattlesnake) can be summarized in one word: wetlands. This association would potentially include all vegetative communities listed above, with the possible exception of alpine tundra. In most areas in the two parks where amphibians and reptiles can be found, meadow, riparian, and/or aquatic habitats would likely be represented to some degree.

As would be expected, all six amphibian species are closely associated with wetland habitats, and four of the six species are found at wetland sites covering the broadest range of elevations we sampled in the region. Extenuating circumstances exist for the other two species; leopard frogs seem to have disappeared (they were never widely distributed in the region in recent history), and bullfrogs are an exotic species persisting only in a highly modified environment (a geothermally heated spring).

Of the six species of reptiles found in the region, three are closely associated with wetland (including riparian, or streamside) habitats: the two species of garter snakes and the rubber boa. In-

Most of the region's amphibians and reptiles can be found near wetlands such as these. We found wandering garter snakes and spotted frogs at this site along the Bechler River in the southeast corner of Yellowstone Park. Ouzel Falls is visible in the background.

deed, the wandering garter snake is sometimes called a "water snake," regularly catching and eating fish, and the valley garter snake often depends heavily on amphibians as a food source. Rubber boas often feed on small mammals, which, in turn, they commonly find in grass and shrub habitats along streams and wetlands. As with the four widespread species of amphibians mentioned above, the wandering garter snake and rubber boa are found at most elevations we sampled, and associated upland habitat types may vary from hot, dry sagebrush to cool subalpine fir forests. Although the valley garter snake is found in both warm sagebrush habitats and in cooler forested areas in the Tetons and southwest corner of Yellowstone, its minimum and maximum elevational distribution is more limited than the other two snake species.

Hill and Moore (1994) further analyzed occurrences of four species of amphibians and reptiles (the blotched tiger salamander, boreal chorus frog, spotted frog, and wandering garter snake) at a to-

Those species not commonly associated with wetlands, including bull snakes, rattlesnakes, and sagebrush lizards, can be found in warmer, drier sagebrush habitat types such as at this site near Deckard Flat along the lower Yellowstone River near Gardiner, Montana. At lower elevations, these species can escape the cold, wet weather of the mountains long enough each year to scratch out a living.

tal of 48 wetland sites on Yellowstone's northern range. They concluded that these species could "potentially be found at [wetland] sites of any size, with any amount of emergent vegetation, and either permanent or ephemeral in nature" and at any elevation for the sites examined. They suspected that the overriding factor determining the presence of these species on Yellowstone's northern range was simply the existence of water for part or all of the year. The boreal toad, leopard frog, bullfrog, valley garter snake, and rubber boa were not evaluated because they either did not occur in the study area or were encountered so infrequently that their occurrence could not be meaningfully evaluated. It seems to us that most amphibians and reptiles that occur at higher elevations in the parks are not continuously distributed but depend on key habitat features, primarily including wetlands and/or geothermally heated areas.

The remaining three species of reptiles (the northern sagebrush lizard, bull snake, and prairie rattlesnake) all share an affinity for relatively hot and dry habitats. These three species can be found together in the lowest elevations of Yellowstone National Park, from near the north entrance at Gardiner, Montana, upstream for at least 5 km (3 mi) on the Yellowstone River. Habitat types in which these species are found include dry, rocky sagebrush flats and ridges. We commonly encountered bull snakes in riparian areas along the Gardner River, but the attraction is probably related to the presence of rodents (their preferred prey). Also, the northern sagebrush lizard can be found in geothermally heated areas, where it can wrest a living from the otherwise prohibitively cold environment.

The Importance of Amphibians and Reptiles

Although amphibians and reptiles do not often receive as much attention as some of the parks' more popular and visible inhabitants, they are important for a number of reasons. First, the aesthetic appreciation of amphibians and reptiles is important for many people. Countless children catch frogs or snakes, and it brings pleasure to see these animals in a natural setting. One of the attractive aspects of amphibians and reptiles is the possibility of observing them for long periods at close range, often without interfering with their normal behavior. They can even be handled briefly in the field and returned gently and quickly to the exact spot where they were found.

Second, amphibians and reptiles are often significant parts of the food web. Many species consume large quantities of insects, other invertebrates, and vertebrate animals, both aquatic and terrestrial. Also, many species provide a food source for predators such as trout, sandhill cranes, great blue herons, red-tail hawks, otters, and other animals including insects, fish, amphibians, reptiles, birds, and mammals. In some areas of North America, the biomass, or total weight, of all amphibians found in an acre of forest may equal or exceed the biomass of all other species of vertebrates combined (Corn and Bury 1990).

Third, these ectothermic animals (that is, animals that gain their body heat from external sources such as the sun) provide ex-

Otters, such as this one in Harlequin Lake in Yellowstone, prey on tiger salamanders, and undoubtedly take other amphibian species as well.

cellent opportunities for scientific research. The use of geothermal features by amphibians and reptiles provides an unusual, natural experiment for examining the effects of heat on the life histories of these animals. The northern sagebrush lizard's use of geothermal areas at elevations that otherwise would be too high for survival in Yellowstone is an excellent example.

Finally, amphibians and reptiles may be good indicators of an ecosystem's health. Even if you are not a big fan of these creatures, just knowing that an ecosystem is healthy enough to support them can provide satisfaction because in many areas amphibians and reptiles have been eliminated due to their sensitivity to pressures from land and water development by humans and to the effects of pollution. Because of amphibians' sensitive skin and the two different stages in their life cycle—one larval, aquatic stage and one terrestrial, adult stage—they can be very sensitive to environmental changes. For instance, amphibian larvae may be exposed to water-borne contaminants such as acid rain. As adults,

The widespread fires of 1988 probably did not have widespread effects on the distribution or abundance of the region's herpetofauna, although a few individuals must have perished. We found nearly 400 spotted frogs in one afternoon in 1991 at our Harlequin Lake amphibian monitoring site, the shore of which, as seen in this photo, burned almost completely.

amphibians prey on insects, which can harbor sublethal amounts of toxic pollutants. When amphibians prey on these insects they can accumulate pollutants in their tissues that may eventually reach lethal levels or impair normal development and reproduction. It is this accumulation of toxic pollutants in the tissues of predators that nearly caused the extinction of the bald eagle and the peregrine falcon in this country. Because most reptiles are also predators, they, too, can suffer from an accumulation of pollutants.

Fire and the Region's Herpetofauna

The fires of 1988 in and around Yellowstone Park affected a large area (for example, nearly 45% of Yellowstone National Park [Schullery 1989]) and were not without precedent. As mentioned earlier, fire has played a key role in shaping plant and animal communities for a long time in the Greater Yellowstone Ecosystem.

Fire is a more frequent visitor to Yellowstone's drier, less forested northern range (every 30 years or so) than it is to the pine, spruce, and fir forests covering much of the rest of the region (on the order of hundreds of years). But eventually most areas will burn (Romme and Despain 1989).

Because of a lack of information on the distribution and abundance of amphibians and reptiles previous to the 1988 fires, it is not possible to directly quantify the effects of the fires on the region's herpetofauna. However, a 1993 comparison of amphibians and reptiles in burned and unburned sites in Yellowstone suggested that the occurrences of some common species (boreal chorus frogs, spotted frogs, and wandering garter snakes) were not significantly altered by the fires (Chris Askey, Southhampton College, Long Island University, personal communication, 1993). Observations we made in 1989 and later are consistent with Askey's findings. In several instances we observed salamanders, frogs, toads, and snakes in areas recently burned. For example, the area around Harlequin Lake near the West Entrance to Yellowstone National Park burned in 1988. In 1991, during a four-hour survey of the lakeshore with Park Resource Management Specialist Craig McClure, we observed over 390 spotted frogs! Certainly, some individual animals must have perished during the fires, and habitat was altered. But our observations show that species of amphibians and reptiles found in areas that burned probably did not experience large changes in their distribution as a result of the extensive 1988 fires.

Declining Amphibian Populations

Presently, many amphibian populations appear to be declining in many places throughout the world. This phenomenon may be part of natural fluctuations in amphibian populations caused by events such as droughts, or humans may be altering global processes, causing warming of the earth, ozone depletion, increased ultraviolet radiation, or acid rain to the point where sensitive animals such as amphibians are harmed. Other human activities that may harm amphibian populations include: habitat alteration, such as draining or filling wetlands; introduction of contaminants to an

Toads were observed in the 1950s near this amphibian monitoring site at Togwotee Pass, east of Grand Teton National Park, but we have yet to observe a single toad here in our six years of searching. We have, however, observed tiger salamanders and boreal chorus frogs. Populations of many species of amphibians appear to be declining in many places throughout the world. The boreal toad, leopard frog, and spotted frog have experienced severe declines elsewhere in their ranges, and in this region only the spotted frog appears to remain near its historical abundance.

area, which either eliminate adult amphibians' food sources or kill or harm amphibians directly; and introduction of exotic species.

Recently, researchers have documented an effect of ultraviolet radiation (UV-B) on the hatching success of eggs from the Cascades frog *(Rana cascade)* and western toad *(Bufo boreas,* of which the boreal toad is a subspecies) in the Cascade Mountain Range of western Oregon (Blaustein et al. 1994). Interestingly, Pacific tree frogs *(Pseudacris regilla)* at the same sites were not affected to the same degree, apparently due to an increased presence of the enzyme photolyase (which repairs damaged genetic material) in the eggs. Cascades frogs and western toads are two species of amphibians that appear to be declining in numbers, and it may be in response to increased ultraviolet radiation due to erosion of the earth's protective ozone layer. In fact, in the experiment, Cascades frog and western toad egg masses that were shielded by UV-B filtering material (like UV-filtering sunglasses) were better off than egg masses left unprotected.

The world's amphibian scientists simply are not yet sure what to make of this perceived decline in amphibian populations in many places around the world. As described above, environmental contaminants may be a major contributing factor in many cases. In Yellowstone and the Tetons, amphibians may be in better shape than in some other areas of the western United States and the world. But unless we determine what is causing the world's amphibian populations to decline, amphibians in this region may encounter trouble in the future. We believe that a decline in abundance and distribution of the boreal toad in this region may already have occurred. In addition, the northern leopard frog can no longer be found in Grand Teton National Park or in some adjacent areas as it was in 1951 (Peterson et al. 1992). However, long-term population data are needed for a clear understanding of trends in amphibian abundance and distribution. Our five years of work in this region have been during a succession of drought years, so our data probably reflect this environmental condition. This fact may heavily influence our present perception of the distribution and abundance of amphibians here.

Populations of some amphibians in other parts of the western United States, including other national parks such as Yosemite National Park (Phillips 1990) and Rocky Mountain National Park (Corn et al. 1989), appear to be declining. The boreal toad and the northern leopard frog have seemingly disappeared from 85% of sites where they occurred historically in Colorado and eastern Wyoming (Corn and Fogelman 1984). The spotted frog is almost gone from the Pacific Northwest coast and seems to be in trouble in the periphery of its range in parts of Washington, Oregon, Nevada, and Utah (Worthing 1993). The U.S. Fish and Wildlife Service is presently considering protecting several species of amphibians under the federal Endangered Species Act of 1973, but agency resources for protecting many species are limited, and delays have occurred in providing legal protection. Even if such protection were given, threats to many species or many populations remain unidentified.

Because amphibians are at least still present, and in some instances quite abundant, in Yellowstone and Grand Teton National Parks, we should monitor these populations now and compare them to populations elsewhere that are either in decline or have disappeared. One of the most frustrating problems with the issue of declining amphibian populations is the lack of historic population data. It may be that amphibian populations in Yellowstone and the Tetons have already declined from what they were decades ago. We fear this may be the case for the boreal toad and northern leopard frog. Baseline data collected now can be used in future evaluations in this same area.

Simplified Key to the Amphibians and Reptiles

THE KEY IS DESIGNED to lead the reader to make a choice between two sets of characteristics. By doing so, the reader eventually moves through each choice in the key to identify a specimen. To use the key for the adult amphibians and reptiles, start at the number "1" and determine if the creature you are examining has smooth, moist skin or skin with warts, *or* if the creature has scaly, dry skin. Once you have made this determination (you have just decided whether the animal is an amphibian or a reptile), go to the number you are directed to next and make another evaluation based on the characteristics described. Remember to refer to the glossary for definitions of unfamiliar terms.

The species of amphibians and reptiles found in the parks should generally be easy to tell apart with the use of a little common sense and this book. The northern leopard frog and the bullfrog are not included in this key because of their extremely limited distribution. For these two species, see the text for a description of what they look like and how to identify them.

Identifying the larval forms of amphibians can, in some instances, be difficult even for trained scientists. Because of this, we have not provided a key to the larval forms of amphibians. For more information and other keys for the larval forms see Nussbaum et al. (1983).

1. Does the animal have smooth, moist skin or skin with warts, and does it lack scales?   amphibian (go to no. 2)

    OR

    Does the animal have scaly, dry skin?   reptile (go to no. 5)

2. Does the animal have a long tail, flat head with a wide mouth, and four legs of similar size, set far apart, with the front legs having four toes and the hind legs having five toes (toes unwebbed)?   blotched tiger salamander (see p. 30)

    OR

    Does the animal lack a tail or have a very short tail, hind legs larger than front legs?   (go to no. 3)

3. Does the animal have small pads at the tips of the toes, no webbing in the hind feet and no warty skin, is brown or light green with darker stripes or elongated spots down the back, and does not exceed 4 cm (1.5 in.) in length?   boreal chorus frog (see p. 58)

    OR

    Does the animal lack toe pads, have webbed hind feet or warty skin, and does not have darker stripes down the back?   (go to no. 4)

4. Does the animal have webbed feet, a dark green or brown color with black spots on the back, and red under the legs?   spotted frog (see p. 69)

    OR

    Does the animal lack webbed hind feet, and does it have light brown, warty skin with a raised swelling behind each eye?   boreal toad (see p. 45)

5. Does the animal have four legs, and does not exceed 13 cm (5 in.) in length?   northern sagebrush lizard (see p. 94)

    OR

    Does the animal lack clearly visible appendages and does it look like a snake?   snake (go to no. 6)

6. Does the animal have a tan ground color with darker patches

along the back, a triangular shaped head with a narrow neck, vertical pupils, and a rattle at the end of the tail?

prairie rattlesnake (see p. 139)

OR

Does the animal lack a triangular shaped head and have no distinct narrowing at the base of the head, and no rattles at the end of the tail?   (go to no. 7)

7. Does the animal have a tan ground color with darker patches along the back?   bull snake (see p. 114)

OR

Is the animal either striped or solid in color, and does it lack a tan ground color with darker patches along the back?

(go to no. 8)

8. Does the animal have a solid color, a blunt tail that resembles the head, small eyes, and smooth scales?

rubber boa (see p. 106)

OR

Does the animal have longitudinal stripes, a pointed tail (compared to the head) and large eyes?   (go to no. 9)

9. Does the animal have a black ground color with distinct, yellow longitudinal stripes and red checkered marks along the sides?   valley garter snake (see p. 131)

OR

Is the animal green brown with yellow longitudinal stripes, and does it lack red sides?   wandering garter snake (see p. 123)

Amphibians
Species Accounts

THE TERM *amphibian* is derived from the Greek words "amphi" meaning double and "bios" meaning life. This term refers to the two-stage life cycle of an amphibian: the larval, aquatic stage and the adult, terrestrial stage. In Yellowstone and the Tetons, amphibians include salamanders, frogs, and toads. Like fish eggs, amphibian eggs lack an external shell and require water or a damp substrate for development. Most amphibians differ from fishes in having four limbs, which are used for locomotion. Their skin is thin and glandular, with a rich blood supply, and it must be kept moist, as opposed to the dry, scaly skin of a reptile. However, like most reptiles and fish, all amphibians are ectothermic, deriving body heat from outside sources.

Amphibian larvae breathe with gills, whereas most adult amphibians breathe with lungs. Both life stages may transfer some oxygen across the skin surface and into the bloodstream.

The greatest number of amphibian species occurs in the tropics (Duellman and Trueb 1986). The number of species generally declines with increasing latitude and can also be limited by moisture availability. For instance, amphibian species richness (the number of species) decreases going from the humid southeastern United States, where the number is high, to the arid western portion of the country, where there are fewer species (Kiester 1971).

Some amphibian species can be abundant locally under the

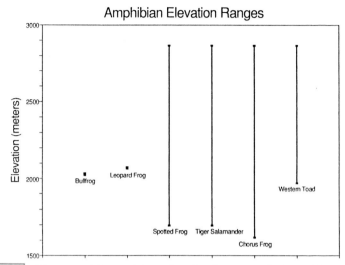

Amphibian Elevation Ranges

All but two of the amphibians found in the region, the leopard frog and the bullfrog, can be found from the lowest elevations in Yellowstone Park near Gardiner, Montana, to the highest elevations in both parks, including up to Togwotee Pass, east of Grand Teton National Park. The leopard frog was historically restricted to the chain of lakes south of Jackson Lake in Jackson Hole, but it can no longer be found there. The bullfrog was introduced and survives in just one location, Kelly Warm Springs and its associated thermal outflows, just outside the eastern border of Grand Teton National Park.

right conditions. But if conditions are dry or otherwise unfavorable, these animals may go unseen for long periods. Some desert amphibians such as spadefoots (or spadefoot "toads"), which have not been confirmed to exist in either park, can live buried underground for months or years of drought before re-emerging overnight to breed following a spring or early summer rainstorm (Bragg 1965).

Six species of amphibians are known to occur in Yellowstone and Grand Teton National Parks. For all but two species, the northern leopard frog and the bullfrog, records exist from the lowest elevations in the region—Gardiner, Montana, at 1600 m (5200 ft) up to at least 2800 m (9200 ft) elevation at Togwotee Pass. The bullfrog (an introduced species) has a severely restricted range in Jackson Hole. The northern leopard frog has not been seen since the 1950s in the few sites where individuals were originally observed in the valley. The remaining four common species of amphibians in the region (the blotched tiger salamander, boreal toad, boreal chorus frog, and spotted frog) can in many places use the same pool or body of water for breeding, but not all pools or water bodies in the region have all four species in them.

Larval amphibians can sometimes be found in abundance in breeding pools in Yellowstone and the Tetons. These pools can range from the shoreline area of a permanent lake or a streamside channel to a shallow vernal pool in a field or forest. The larvae of frogs and toads are called tadpoles. Blotched tiger salamander larvae are called "larvae," but some sexually mature, larval tiger salamanders are referred to as "axolotls," or "paedomorphs." Tiger salamander larvae are carnivorous and have external gills and four legs. Tadpoles are usually herbivorous and have only a tail until they approach metamorphosis, when legs sprout and, after further development, they crawl onto land as frogs or toads. Larval tiger salamanders resemble the adult form and are distinct from the tadpoles. The distinction between the tadpoles of the frogs and toads is more difficult (see the individual species account).

Adult male frogs and toads sometimes have breeding calls to attract females of the same species to suitable breeding sites. Breeding occurs in the spring for all of this region's amphibians, and the loud and persistent call of the boreal chorus frog heard regionwide at some time between April and July is a sure sign that the spring season is upon us. This is the only species of amphibian found in both parks whose call you can expect to hear consistently each spring.

Blotched Tiger Salamander
Ambystoma tigrinum melanostictum

Adult tiger salamanders cannot be confused with any other of the region's amphibians, all of which are frogs or toads. We have occasionally heard people mistake these animals for lizards. They differ greatly from lizards by having smooth, nonscaly skin, clawless toes, and relatively slow movement. Adults generally have a dark ground color with lighter marbled color patterns along the back and sides, such as this animal observed at an amphibian monitoring site near Slough Creek in the northeast corner of Yellowstone Park. This species is common where found and is widely distributed throughout both parks.

The blotched tiger salamander is the subspecies of tiger salamander that occurs in the Greater Yellowstone Ecosystem. Tiger salamanders are members of the mole salamander family (Ambystomatidae). Larval tiger salamanders that do not transform into adults but breed in their juvenile (neotenic) form are commonly referred as "paedomorphs" or by the Aztec name of "axolotl."

Description

ADULT. An adult blotched tiger salamander has a broad, somewhat flattened head with a large, terminal mouth and two small, protruding eyes. The four limbs are similar in length with the front legs having four toes each and the hind legs having five toes each. This species may have intercostal grooves (vertical grooves along the side of the body between the front and hind limbs). Coloration can range from a light olive or brown background to nearly solid black with only a hint of brown or green. Individuals often have yellow blotches or streaks, especially on the back and sides, which give this salamander its name. In the adult form the tail is rounded, and larvae or recently transformed adults may have a ridge or fin on the top and bottom, which helps propel them through the water. Length of adults from head to tail ranges up to 23 cm (9 in.), with the tail composing nearly one-half that length (Carpenter 1953a). Carpenter (1953a) found that adults captured in aquatic habitats were larger than adults captured on land. We have also observed this phenomenon in the Lamar Valley of Yellowstone and in a pond near Togwotee Pass. Males have a bulbous vent, longer tails and longer, stouter hind limbs than females (Nussbaum et al. 1983, Stebbins 1985).

LARVAE. In contrast to adults, the larvae of the blotched tiger salamander have wider heads, uniform color, and large, feathery external gills, which are located on either side of the body behind the

31

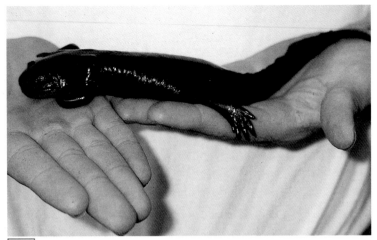

Some tiger salamanders can be quite large and uniformly dark in color, such as this individual captured at Togwotee Pass, east of Grand Teton National Park. Notice that although the animal has transformed into an adult and lacks external gills typical of larval salamanders, it retains its ridged, fin-like tail for propulsion through water. In other areas, complete transformations result in attainment of a rounded tail on the adults, which are up to half the size of this specimen.

The larval form of the tiger salamander is easy to differentiate from other larval amphibians in the region because of its large, flat head with large external gills on each side and long, tapered body with four widely spaced (though small) limbs. They are generally a dark, uniform green or brown color and lack the light marbled coloration of the adults. This species has been the focus of medical research because of the ability of some individuals to breed in their larval form and not transform into adults.

head and in front of the forelimbs (the forelimbs may be reduced in size compared to the adult). Larvae also have a ridge or fin on the tail. Lengths of larvae can range from 1 cm (0.4 in.) just after hatching to over 20 cm (8 in.) in this region. Although larvae at Ice Lake in Yellowstone (near Gardiner, Montana) are comparable in length to terrestrial adults, they weigh nearly twice as much as the adults (Hill 1995). All larvae we have observed in Yellowstone and the Tetons are light to dark olive green. The difference between the tiger salamander larvae and the other amphibian larvae (all of them tadpoles) is simple; tiger salamander larvae have a wide head with large external, feathery gills on either side of the head, and they commonly appear similar to the adult form, with a long tail and, when present, four appendages widely spaced on the body.

SIMILAR SPECIES.   Although there are no other species of salamanders in the Greater Yellowstone Ecosystem, salamanders are sometimes confused with lizards. However, the difference between these two very different animals is rather easily learned. The tiger salamander has a smooth, moist skin; rounded features; and no claws. A lizard has scaly, dry skin; sharper features; and true claws. In Yellowstone and the Tetons, these two animals are generally found in different habitats, with the salamander occurring in water or moist areas associated with ground burrows, and the sagebrush lizard being found near thermal areas and/or in areas strewn with rocks or logs in relatively warm, dry microclimates. During the period of wetness provided by a cool summer rainstorm, blotched tiger salamanders can occasionally be found in sagebrush habitats with surface water nearby. During this cool, wet time, any lizards—which could occur in rocky areas nearby— would be in hiding.

Distribution

The tiger salamander is the most widely distributed of all North American salamanders, ranging from British Columbia and Alberta, Canada, south to northern Florida, excluding New England and much of the west coast (Stebbins 1985). It is the only salamander known to occur in Yellowstone or Grand Teton National

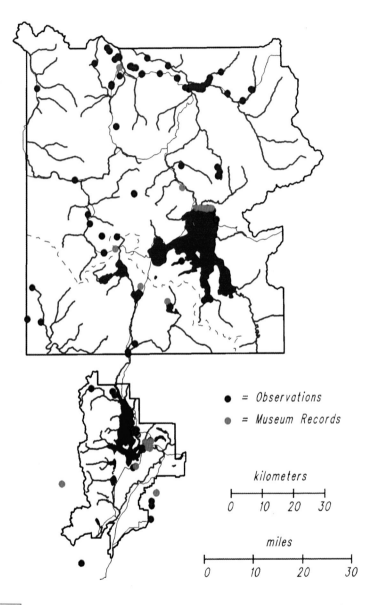

● = *Observations*

● = *Museum Records*

kilometers

0   10   20   30

miles

0   10   20   30

Tiger salamanders occur in a variety of locations from the warm, arid northern range of Yellowstone to the cool mountain wetlands of the Tetons to the south. Many places in both parks remain unsampled.

Parks. The distribution of blotched tiger salamanders appears to be widespread throughout both parks. It was the most widely distributed of five amphibian and reptile species examined on Yellowstone's northern range in 1992 and 1993 (Hill and Moore 1994). Black (1970) reported that this species continues its range from the northern portion of Yellowstone northward (and down in elevation) into most of Montana. Baxter and Stone (1985) also reported that this salamander can be found continuously throughout virtually all of Wyoming, and Nussbaum et al. (1983) reported that the range of tiger salamanders includes portions of eastern and northern Idaho.

Blotched tiger salamanders occur over a wide range of elevations. They can be found at the lowest elevations in either park, including Slide Lake at 1740 m (5710 ft), just a short distance southeast of Gardiner, Montana, at the North Entrance to Yellowstone. We also have collected this species as larvae and as adults at 2800 m (9200 ft) elevation at Togwotee Pass, east of Jackson Hole. In their book on the fishes of Yellowstone, Varley and Schullery (1983) point out that in Yellowstone National Park this species has not been seen above 2500 m (8200 ft) elevation.

Abundance/Status
Tiger salamanders appear to be common to abundant throughout their range in both parks.

Natural History
Fortunately for those of us interested in the natural history of this species in the area, Steven Hill of Montana State University studied blotched tiger salamanders on Yellowstone's northern range in 1992 and 1993 for his master's degree (Hill 1995). He collected detailed data on movements of salamanders at Ice Lake Reservoir near Gardiner, Montana, by completely encircling the lake with low fencing and trapping animals moving to and from the lake. This old, small reservoir was created to provide a supply of ice for keeping food cool in ice boxes before modern refrigeration was widely available. But despite its chilly name, this body of water is likely to attain higher water temperatures for longer periods of time than most other permanent water bodies in either park be-

We have found tiger salamanders to be common in glacial ponds such as this one—one of our amphibian monitoring sites—near Slough Creek in the Lamar Valley in the northeastern corner of Yellowstone. In springtime this site is open water, without the emergent vegetation seen in this photo. As summer progresses, the water level drops and vegetation encroaches, making salamanders and other animals harder to see. We have also seen chorus frogs, spotted frogs, and wandering garter snakes at this site.

cause it is the lowest elevation, permanent lake in either park. Therefore, the timing of life history events for tiger salamanders here is likely to be earlier than in most other places in either park.

HABITAT.   Tiger salamanders occur in a wide variety of habitats, including quiet waters in lakes, ponds, rivers, and streams in sagebrush flats, grasslands, meadows, and/or forests (Stebbins 1985). Adults spend a great deal of their time in burrows but return to the water for breeding. They are very adaptable; park maintenance personnel have even reported seeing larval salamanders underground in portions of water drainage systems serving the Lake Area and other areas in Yellowstone, and in the Colter Bay area in the Tetons. Of the 48 aquatic habitat sites examined on Yellowstone's northern range in 1992 and 1993, the 31 sites where blotched tiger salamanders were observed were significantly deeper (average depth of 158 cm [5 ft]) than the remaining 17 sites where they were not observed (average depth of 41 cm [16 in.])(Hill and Moore 1994).

Temperature appears to be an important influence on micro-habitat (for example, the square meter or yard within a pond being used by an animal) selection in larval and adult tiger salamanders in aquatic environments. Tiger salamanders in a breeding pond migrate daily from shallows during the day to deep water at night in search of the warmest water temperatures (Heath 1975). In the Tetons, Carpenter (1953a) observed that larval salamanders gathered together in aggregations and, after being disturbed, returned to reaggregate, probably because of the temperature characteristics of that site. Tiger salamander larvae, adults, and axolotls regulate their body temperature in high altitude environments, selecting the warmest water temperatures available as long as they do not exceed 27°C (81°F); water temperatures at high altitude salamander sites rarely exceed 25–30°C (77–86°F) (Heath 1975). Larvae appear to control body temperatures more closely than adults in aquatic environments, and salamanders from all life stages select temperatures between 24–26°C (75–80°F) when provided with a sufficiently wide range of temperatures to choose from.

ACTIVITY PATTERNS.   Tiger salamander adults probably hibernate in burrows during the winter and then migrate to breeding sites in the spring. Adult tiger salamanders can be found hundreds of meters (yards) from any surface water. From just a few adult tiger salamanders to hundreds of thousands of adults have been observed moving across sagebrush flats after a summer thunderstorm. We know of at least six areas where salamander migrations of some magnitude have been observed: Little America Flats, which lies between the Yellowstone River bridge and the Lamar River bridge on the Tower – Northeast Entrance road in Yellowstone; the Hoodoos near Africa Lake on the Norris – Mammoth road; the Swan Lake Flats area south of Mammoth in Yellowstone; along the banks of the Yellowstone River in Hayden Valley; in the Colter Bay area in the Tetons; and along the road from Signal Mountain to Jenny Lake near the Potholes region in the Tetons. Five of these six areas are associated with roads. Of course, roads are not required for salamander migrations to occur, but along roads is where most observations are commonly made because that is where people spend most of their time. Carpenter (1953a) observed that, in the Jackson Hole valley, migrating adult salamanders were almost always associated with sagebrush habitats, and he rarely found terrestrial, adult tiger salamanders in forested areas in the Tetons.

In the Lamar Valley of Yellowstone, the general direction of these migrations in the summertime appears to be from south to north. In 1935, Pierson (1950 *cited in* Turner 1955) reported a migration of what appeared to be thousands of salamanders crossing the highway in a northerly direction about 2 km (1.5 mi) east of Tower Junction.

The size of these migrations may range from a few individuals (Roy Wood, Yellowstone National Park, personal communication, 1989) to many thousands (Varley and Schullery 1983). After a rainstorm on a June evening in 1985, grizzly bear researchers Stephen and Marilyn French (independent researchers, personal communication, 1989) observed many thousands of adult salamanders on the road as far as they could see in either direction.

On an August afternoon in 1989 at a pond at Little America Flats, we were fortunate enough to observe adult salamanders as they emerged from underground burrows as a thundershower threatened and it rained lightly. When we inspected several ground squirrel burrows on the sagebrush-covered hillside to the south and west of the pond, we were excited to find an adult tiger salamander sitting at the opening of five out of the eight burrows examined. Of the several burrows examined farther away on the south side of the road, none had salamanders in them.

One of the earliest descriptions of any of Yellowstone's herpetofauna is of the blotched tiger salamander (or what is referred to in the account as a "black lizzard"). Captain DeLacy (1876) wrote of his trip in 1863 up the south fork of the Snake River into part of what was to become Yellowstone National Park. On the seventh of September, he and his party camped in "a small dry prairie" with "a damp place in the center" north and east of Shoshone Lake.

As a thunderstorm loomed one afternoon in mid-August, we observed adult tiger salamanders at the mouths of five out of eight animal burrows examined, including this one, in the Lamar Valley in the northeast corner of Yellowstone. In this and in several other places throughout the region, tiger salamanders migrate by the hundreds of thousands following rainstorms in midsummer. Although some degree of movement occurs every year, large migrations are observed only in certain years, for reasons yet unknown.

As soon as the camp-fires were lit, thousands of black lizzards [sic] came forth from the woods, and the whole country was alive with them, doubtless attracted by the light. They made their way directly toward the fires, and rushed right into them by the dozens, and burned up. There seemed to be no end to their number. After supper I sat down on a log and watched them. I noticed that many would get right into the hot ashes and take some time to scratch, and doubtless suffer great pain. As I am naturally kind-hearted, I just got a crooked stick, and whenever I saw one of them come up and balance himself on his forepaws, looking for a good opening for a young lizzard, I raked him right into the flame, and saved him any further trouble. They continued to annoy us all night, getting into our blankets, and making themselves generally unpleasant until morning.

It rained heavily during the night. . . .

This account of salamanders freely entering lethally hot environments is not unprecedented. In fact, the Greek and Latin term "salamandra" refers to a mythical, lizardlike animal that is supposedly able to live in fire. Curiously, we have also received reports of blotched tiger salamanders crawling directly into scalding hot water in hot springs in Yellowstone. And Turner (1955) observed a salamander "cooked" to death on very hot ground near a thermal feature at Beach Springs on the edge of Yellowstone Lake.

Our data and those of Carpenter (1953a) show that migrations in both parks are most likely to occur after a rainstorm in the spring and late summer and that movements in general are most likely to occur at night. For example, of the approximately 400 individual movements of salamanders to and from Ice Lake Reservoir, 91% were within 24 hours after a rainstorm, and 99% were at night (Steven Hill, personal communication, 1994).

Migrations to Ice Lake Reservoir in Yellowstone in 1993 began on or before April 9, just after winter ice and snow had melted, with the largest immigration event of 27 individuals occurring on May 15 (Hill 1995). Emigration of salamanders from the lake in 1993 began in earnest by early July, with 29 individuals emigrating on July 24 and 33 individuals emigrating on August 5. Approximately half of the individuals emigrating on August 5 had recently metamorphosed from the larval to the adult form.

FEEDING HABITS.   The tiger salamander is carnivorous and known for its varied diet and ravenous appetite. Similar to young fish, the larvae eat zooplankton (microscopic aquatic animals), aquatic insect larvae, other invertebrates, tadpoles, and sometimes other salamander larvae. In the Tetons, larval salamanders seem to preferentially prey on smaller boreal chorus frog tadpoles (5–8.5 mm [about 0.25–0.34 in.] body length) rather than larger ones (Woodward and Mitchell 1992). Adults eat earthworms, insects, and occasionally small vertebrates (Nussbaum et al. 1983). They truly are the tigers of the amphibian world! In the absence of fish, neotenic salamanders may fill the ecological role of fish in the food chain and may be important in determining the relationships among other aquatic organisms.

ENEMIES/DEFENSE.   A wide variety of animals prey on tiger salamanders, including great blue herons, sandhill cranes, ravens, garter snakes, trout, otters, and badgers (Carpenter 1953a), and coyotes and bobcats (Webb and Rouche 1971). Varley and Schullery (1983) pointed out that, with some exceptions, salamanders are generally not found in water bodies harboring significant fish populations. In fact, the presence of tiger salamanders in a lake or pond generally indicates to fish biologists that the lake or pond is fishless. Regrettably, by introducing non-native fishes into fishless lakes in Yellowstone earlier in this century, managers may have harmed blotched tiger salamander populations in their native habitat. We now know that, at least in national parks, it is best to leave a lake or stream fishless if it was that way naturally.

Tiger salamanders are especially vulnerable during their migrations. Wuerthner (1991) reported that otters may feed heavily on migrating salamanders along the lower Lamar River. Automobiles also may kill many salamanders when they are crossing roads. Roy Wood (Yellowstone National Park, personal communication, 1989) found that 55 out of 93 adult salamanders he observed on the road after a rainstorm had been crushed by the wheels of automobiles (he undoubtedly missed counting many more survivors that crossed the road successfully before his arrival). Varley and Schullery (1983) reported that during mass migrations the road can become slick from salamanders being squashed under the tires of vehicles.

Leeches have been observed on salamanders in the Jackson Hole area (Carpenter 1953a). He concluded that leeches "prey extensively on adult and larval salamanders." Steven Hill (Montana State University, personal communication, 1993) also observed leeches on salamanders in the Lamar Valley and on Mt. Everts in Yellowstone.

An important survival strategy for tiger salamanders may simply be that they produce large numbers of individuals so that even if a population experiences high levels of predation, many salamanders will remain to reproduce the following year. Tiger salamanders also employ an interesting behavioral defense strategy which may help them avoid predators, called aposematic (literally: conspicuous, or warning) behavior. Carpenter (1955) observed that five individuals out of twelve salamanders located in Jackson Hole on a rainy, late July night in 1951, ". . . stopped, spread and arched its hind legs, raised its tail almost to the vertical and then waived it back and forth." He remarked that the effect of waving the tail with its black and yellow pattern was quite spectacular, and speculated that such behavior could serve to frighten small predators and startle large predators long enough to allow escape.

REPRODUCTION/DEVELOPMENT.   Adult tiger salamanders migrate to breeding ponds soon after the snow melts in springtime. This movement varies according to the elevation of a particular breeding site but generally occurs between April and June. After a swarming courtship ritual, the male deposits a packet of sperm (called a spermatophore) on the pond substrate. The female then picks up the spermatophore in her cloaca, and fertilization occurs internally (Baxter and Stone 1985). We have observed up to 20 fertilized eggs attached to vegetation in shallow water at several locations in the parks, and in other parts of their range an individual female may lay over 7,000 eggs (Nussbaum et al. 1983). At Ice Lake Reservoir, a total of about 920 eggs were laid on minnow trap lines in 11 different instances between April 23 and May 12, 1993 (Steven Hill, personal communication, 1994).

After a two- to four-week incubation period, the eggs hatch; larvae are about 1 cm (0.4 in.) in length (Nussbaum et al. 1983). A few weeks after the individuals hatch, front legs appear, followed by the emergence of hind legs (Turner 1951). This order of appearance of the limbs is opposite that of the other amphibians found in the region, none of which are salamanders.

In some situations, the larvae may not transform into the adult life stage to breed but instead breed in the sexually mature larval form (as axolotls). This remarkable feat is termed *paedogenesis*. Some untransformed salamanders were found to be gravid in April 1993 in Ice Lake (Steven Hill, personal communication, 1994). In Ice Lake, of the 15 large larvae captured from May to September

Tiger salamander eggs are usually distinguishable from eggs of other amphibian species in the region. Salamanders attach their eggs singly along vegetation in shallow water. This behavior is similar only to the chorus frog, whose eggs are smaller.

1993, most if not all individuals were sexually mature. Other times larvae may overwinter two or possibly more years before transforming into adults (Turner 1951; Baxter and Stone 1985; Steven Hill, personal communication, 1994). Varley and Schullery (1983) suggested that the elevation of breeding ponds in Yellowstone may be related to whether or not some larvae transform into the adult phase to breed. This suggestion may be true, but we have seen metamorphosed adult salamanders at our highest elevation sample site at Togwotee Pass east of the Tetons at about 2800 m (9200 ft) elevation. The propensity for paedomorphism in some populations of tiger salamanders is likely to be partly genetically influenced (that is, some populations will tend to be paedomorphic more than others no matter what environmental conditions they are faced with). But paedomorphism is also influenced by other abiotic factors, such as the permanency of water at a breeding site (for example, if water at the site dries up, most individuals would tend to transform or else they would perish). This highly unusual and variable metamorphic behavior has stimulated biologists to seek an explanation for such behavior. Voluminous research publications on this subject have appeared. The knowledge gained might benefit humans directly.

Boreal Toad
Bufo boreas boreas

Adult toads can be distinguished from other adult amphibians in the region by warty skin (with prominent parotoid glands behind each eye), light brown color, and white stripe running down the length of the back. They travel in short hops, rather than the leaping action typical of the spotted frog, and can often be found far from surface water, as this animal was near the south entrance to Yellowstone Park. Toads can be common where found, and occur in widely varying habitats in both parks. Their abundance appears reduced from forty years ago.

The boreal toad is the subspecies of the western toad found in Yellowstone and Grand Teton National Parks. It is the only true toad (Family Bufonidae) found in either of the parks.

Description

ADULTS.   Adult boreal toads range in size from 55 to 125 mm (2 to 5 in.) in length (Nussbaum et al. 1983). The maximum size of females is greater than that of males. Boreal toads have a stocky, or plump, body and travel by short hops or by "walking," as opposed to the leaping movements of frogs. The head of a boreal toad is short and blunt, and the eyes have horizontal pupils. The toad's hind feet are moderately webbed, with relatively short toes. Each foot has two cornified tubercles, or hard brown protuberances, on the outside of the bottom of the foot near the heel. These tubercles are used by the toad for digging in loose or sandy soil (Nussbaum et al. 1983). The ground color of boreal toads varies from brown to gray or green. There are dark brown or black spots and a distinct, thin, light-colored stripe running along the length of the middle of their backs. The ventral surface is lightly colored with dark mottling. Toads may darken or lighten with decreasing or increasing temperature, respectively. Their skin is relatively thick, with a bumpy or "warty" texture on the dorsal side of the animal, with thinner and smoother skin under the belly and legs. The bumps on their backs are concentrations of poison glands. The two largest brown "bumps," which exist behind each eye on the back of the toad, are called parotoid glands. The skin of the toad may appear dry as they may spend a considerable amount of time away from surface water.

During the breeding season, the males develop conspicuous, thickened dark areas on the upper surface of their thumbs. These thickenings are called *nuptial pads*, and they help the male hold onto the female during *amplexus* (the mating position). Later in the year, these pads may lose their color and thickness and become relatively difficult to see.

Toad tadpoles can be difficult to distinguish from spotted frog and chorus frog tadpoles because the larvae of all three species have a similar body shape. The easiest way to differentiate the toad tadpole is by its uniformly black color and small size. Also, toad tadpoles will often swim in huge aggregations in shallow water.

JUVENILES. Juvenile boreal toads generally look like smaller versions of the adults but they may have reddish spots on their bodies and yellow spots on the underside of their feet.

TADPOLES. Boreal toad larvae are commonly known as *tadpoles*. They have a rounded shape and generally do not attain a large size. Seven tadpoles averaged nearly 12 mm (0.5 in.) in length in a pond in Jackson Hole on July 7, 1951, and the maximum size recorded for tadpoles in Jackson Hole on August 14 of the same year was 38 mm (1.5 in.) in length (Carpenter 1953a). During most of their development they are completely black, so much so that even in direct sunlight it can be difficult to discern surface features of the toad tadpole.

SIMILAR SPECIES. Boreal toad tadpoles could be confused with young spotted frog tadpoles; the spotted frog tadpole can be very dark shortly after hatching (Turner 1958a). Adult toads might occasionally be confused with adult spotted frogs, which also have bumps on their skin. However, spotted frogs have a smoother skin than toads, are generally green with black spots, have heavily webbed feet, and no large parotoid glands behind the eyes. Boreal toads also have a distinctive musky odor that probably originates from skin gland secretions (Baxter and Stone 1985).

Distribution

The boreal toad is generally found in the western half of the North American continent, from southeastern Alaska south to northern New Mexico in the Rocky Mountains, and west from there to the Pacific Ocean (Stebbins 1985). It is widely distributed throughout Yellowstone and the Tetons, from the lowest elevations of both parks up to about 2865 m (9400 ft) near Togwotee Pass (at least historically), nearly 45 km (30 mi) east of Jackson Hole and Grand Teton National Park. Outside of the Greater Yellowstone Ecosystem, this species is not found at lower elevations east of western Wyoming (Baxter and Stone 1985), western Montana, and central Colorado (Stebbins 1985). It is found to the west throughout most of Idaho. The boreal toad is one of only two amphibians or reptiles (the other being the wandering garter snake) for which we have a recorded observation high in the Teton Range (in upper Death Canyon, on the west side of Jackson Hole.) Some other species of amphibians and reptiles probably occur there but have been never been recorded.

Abundance/Status

Boreal toads in Yellowstone and the Tetons can be locally common to abundant. This toad species appears to have declined in both distribution and abundance in some portions of its range in the western United States. In Colorado, eastern Wyoming, and eastern Utah, this once abundant and common species can no longer be found in about 85% of the sites where it occurred historically (Corn et al. 1989).

Even in the Greater Yellowstone Ecosystem, this species appears to be less abundant and widespread than it was historically. In Jackson Hole, Carpenter (1953a) called the boreal toad "the most wide-spread amphibian in the region — it is found in almost

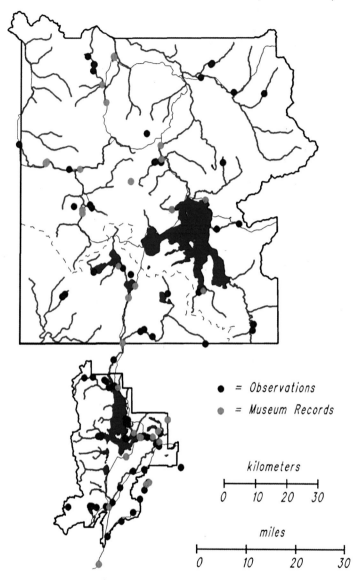

● = *Observations*

● = *Museum Records*

kilometers

0   10   20   30

miles

0   10   20   30

Boreal toads occur in a variety of locations from the warm, arid northern range of Yellowstone to the cool mountain wetlands of the Tetons to the south. Recently, however, we have only found this species in Yellowstone breeding at geothermally influenced sites, and boreal toads may have declined in abundance over the last 40 years. Many places in both parks remain unsampled.

every locality and in a great variety of habitats." Carpenter (1954) also found about as many adult toads at one site downstream of Jackson Lake Dam in 1951 as we have seen in both parks in three years of intensive searching. Habitat alteration may be proposed as a partial explanation for boreal toad declines in Jackson Hole. Construction and operation of the dam at the outlet of Jackson Lake was completed subsequent to data collected by Carpenter (1954). Water is stored behind the dam during the normally high water flows of springtime. Reductions in springtime flood flows, coupled with mechanical stream-channel confinement, probably greatly reduced the effects of natural flood events on the wetlands that toads depended on for breeding sites, and altered or destroyed much of the habitat where Carpenter (1954) collected most of his data. Indeed, Carpenter himself had difficulty even recognizing his old study site when he visited the channelized river below the dam with us in 1992.

Turner (1955) alluded to the abundance of the toad in Yellowstone when he mentioned "the large number of crushed toads which may be noted on the roads around Fishing Bridge and Lake during July and August." But we have found only two toads in this area in the last six years. On Yellowstone's northern range in 1992 and 1993, the boreal toad was found less often (at only 3 of the 48 sites examined) than the other 4 species of amphibians and reptiles observed (Hill and Moore 1994). Our observations, along with comparisons with data collected 40 years ago and consultations with others, including Drs. Carpenter and Turner, show that the boreal toad may be less widespread and abundant in the Greater Yellowstone Ecosystem today than it was 40 years ago. We must note, however, that we have conducted most of our research during a series of drought years and some areas in the region still support successfully reproducing populations of toads. Also, we have seen dozens to thousands of tadpoles and recently metamorphosed individuals at some of these sites.

Natural History

HABITAT.   Boreal toads occur in a variety of habitats. They apparently hibernate terrestrially in burrows or cavities (Paul Bartelt, Idaho State University, personal communication, 1993). We have

Toads are commonly found near warm, shallow water areas with adjacent large meadows, such as this amphibian monitoring site east of the Snake River at Yellowstone's South Entrance. We have observed adults foraging and breeding at this site, and we have observed tens of thousands of tadpoles in this geothermally influenced stream channel as they were transforming into adults. Interestingly, most sites in the region where toads occur are geothermally influenced. We have also observed tiger salamanders, spotted frogs, chorus frogs, and wandering garter snakes near here.

found them breeding in large and small lakes, beaver ponds, temporary ponds, slow-moving streams, and backwater channels of rivers. The water chemistry at most of the current breeding sites we have observed is distinctive. It generally has a high pH [> 8.0], high conductivity, and high acid-neutralizing capacity, which all means that, among other things, the water is probably resistant to any risk of acidification. In Yellowstone, all five of the breeding sites we know of are geothermally influenced.

ACTIVITY PATTERNS.   Adult toads in this region probably migrate from hibernation sites to breeding sites any time from May to early July. We have observed: considerable interindividual variation (at least two months) in timing of breeding activity, even at the same site; active toads during both the daytime and at night (especially when it was raining); and mating during the day.

After breeding is completed (see section on reproduction), toads may disperse considerable distances away from water (Turner 1955; Paul Bartelt, Idaho State University, personal communication, 1993). In this region we have found toads in riparian areas adjacent to streams, wet meadows, sagebrush meadows, and coniferous forests. We observed one adult in a sagebrush meadow over 400 m (yd) from the nearest surface water on a June morning at 10:00 a.m. in the Hayden Valley of Yellowstone. Baxter and Stone (1985) reported that toads will move far from water more commonly at night and that they may feed all night long. As mentioned above, the skin of western toads tends to be drier than most amphibians, especially along the back and sides of the animal, which are exposed to the desiccating effects of the sun and wind. The ability of western toads to remain away from surface water for relatively long periods of time is due to their drier skin and higher tolerance of water loss (Thorson and Svihla 1943). Western toads have thinner, more permeable skin on their underbelly and thighs. An individual toad may be able to find a puddle mere millimeters (or fractions of an inch) deep and absorb enough water through this permeable skin to rehydrate and store additional water for continued travel in drier habitats. On the nearby Targhee National Forest, Paul Bartelt (personal communication, 1993) attached miniature radio transmitters to boreal toads and determined that females may move up to 2.4 km away from the breeding site within several weeks, whereas males may remain closer to the breeding site. Adult toads with transmitters spent the majority of their time in burrows or under logs. Several toads may congregate under rocks prior to hibernation (Ray Clark and Paul Bartelt, personal communication, 1993).

FEEDING HABITS.   Nussbaum et al. (1983) reported that "Western toads eat virtually every kind of flying insect in addition to spiders, crayfish, sowbugs and earthworms." Ants may compose the majority of the diet in some areas (Campbell 1970), including the Targhee National Forest (Stephen Sullivan, Idaho State University, personal communication, 1994), in addition to moths, beetles, and other insects. Turner (1955) collected four toads along the banks of the Madison River in Yellowstone on the night of May

20, 1954, and all four individuals had been feeding almost exclusively on ants. They also had ingested numerous small stones. Boreal toads also will eat small vertebrates, and we have even heard a report from Idaho of a large toad trying unsuccessfully to eat a small rubber boa at night (Al Larson, Boise, Idaho, personal communication, 1993).

ENEMIES/DEFENSE.   Boreal toads and tadpoles may be preyed upon by a variety of predators, including insects, garter snakes, ravens, coyotes, raccoons, and badgers (Carpenter 1953a, Nussbaum et al. 1983, Corn 1993, Leonard et al. 1993). Because adult female boreal toads can produce thousands of eggs and offspring, it stands to reason that a lot of these offspring end up as food for many of the region's predators. We have found recently transformed toads in the stomachs of wandering garter snakes near the South Entrance of Yellowstone. We also found the skull and skin of an adult toad along the shore of a beaver pond in the Tetons. Corn (1993) concluded that ravens will capture and skin a toad (presumably to remove the unpalatable skin glands) before eating it. Carpenter (1953a) reported that a badger in the Jackson Hole area was found to have six adult boreal toads in its stomach. We also observed leeches on the undersurface of an adult toad in a beaver pond along the Snake River in Grand Teton National Park.

One of the primary means of defense for boreal toads is their poison glands. These glands contain a toxic substance that the toad secretes to defend itself from many (but not all) potential predators. Although you cannot get warts from handling a toad, you should be careful not to touch your eyes after handling a toad because the toxins in the toad's skin may be irritating.

REPRODUCTION/DEVELOPMENT.   Adult toads in this region probably migrate to breeding sites anytime from May to July. Male boreal toads are not commonly known to call to attract females, although they are capable of making noise and do so on occasion when near other males in a breeding pool (Nussbaum et al. 1983; Paul Bartelt, personal communication, 1993) and when handled. However, in Montana, male toads were observed responding to other male toads' vocalizations, and the observers concluded that

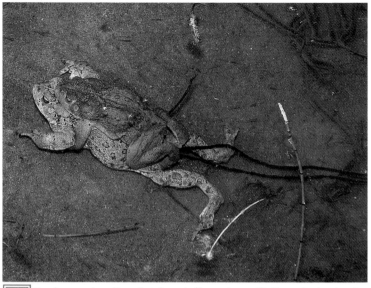

Toads reproduce like other frogs in the region, with the male clasping the female from behind in a position called amplexus. A pair of toads may remain in this position for hours, alternately sinking to the muddy bottom to release eggs in pulses and rising to the water surface to rest and breathe. The female extrudes eggs in two separate strings emerging simultaneously, with eggs encased in separate, gelatin-sheathed strands, which swell in size upon contact with the water.

females may also be attracted (Black and Brunson 1971). Male toads may outnumber females in a breeding pond by four to one (Nussbaum et al. 1983). Females can lay an average of 12,000 eggs per individual (maximum 16,000). Eggs are laid in two long strings of individual eggs encased in a gelatinous sheath, or flexible tube, on the silty bottoms of shallow pools. Time until hatching is probably less than two weeks in the Greater Yellowstone Ecosystem.

We had the good fortune to observe two breeding pairs of boreal toads in late morning on May 16, 1993, in an old river oxbow 0.5 km (0.3 mi) east of the Snake River near the South Entrance Ranger Station in Yellowstone Park. The two pairs of toads were about 5 m (yd) apart in water 10–15 cm (4–6 in.) deep. In each pair, the male grabbed the female immediately behind the front legs in a position called *amplexus.* A third, unattached male toad attempted to intrude on the first breeding pair of toads seen but was

After being laid, the strands of eggs often intertwine with emergent vegetation, or they are strewn randomly across the muddy bottom of a shallow wetland site. Boreal toad eggs are among the more visible types of egg masses to observe in the region.

Toad tadpoles have often been observed together by the tens of thousands in shallow water areas at breeding sites. We had the good fortune to observe this huge aggregation of young boreal toads, with animals piled two or three deep in some places, as they transformed from the larval, tadpole form into the adult form at our amphibian monitoring site near Yellowstone's South Entrance. Most of the animals in this photograph were simply miniature versions of adults, but many had small tail stubs left. Other individuals, which looked to be almost as far along in their development into adults as their now-terrestrial counterparts, were swimming in nearby shallow water as tadpoles normally do.

driven off by forceful kicking of both toads in the pair. One minute after the encounter, the female extruded about 20 cm (8 in.) of eggs from her vent. The toads alternately came to the surface for 1–2 minutes, apparently to breath, and then submerged themselves for 3–4 minutes. Upon submergence, the female contracted her abdomen repeatedly, rested, and then continued with the contractions another one to three times during each submergence. The male moved his pelvis up and down simultaneously with the contractions of the female. Eggs emerged from each of the females in a continuous double string and swelled, more than doubling in size after about 5 minutes in the water.

Toad tadpoles may occur together in huge aggregations. We observed an intermittent band of boreal toad tadpoles in a small, geothermally heated stream channel near the South Entrance to Yellowstone. This band of tadpoles averaged 0.5 m (1.6 ft) wide and was dozens of meters (yards) long. We could not estimate how many thousands of tadpoles were present. Nussbaum et al. (1983) observed one column of western toad tadpoles in a mountain lake in the Pacific Northwest to be 300 m (yd) long and averaged about 1 m wide. There may be several advantages to aggregation behavior in tadpoles. Tadpoles swimming in large groups may be churning up sediment upon which they will feed. Also, water temperatures in the midst of these aggregations can be 2–3°C (3–5°F) warmer than surrounding water (Nussbaum et al. 1983), thus speeding development of individuals.

Metamorphosis of boreal toad tadpoles has been observed at considerably varying times of year in this region. We observed thousands of transforming toads 0.5 km (0.3 mi) east of the South Entrance of Yellowstone at a geothermally heated site as early as mid-June of 1991 – unexpectedly early in the year. At another site along Alum Creek in Hayden Valley in Yellowstone where geothermal activity also was present, we observed recently transformed toads in mid-August. We also observed transformed toads in a beaver pond at Schwabacher Landing along the Snake River in the Tetons in mid-August 1992. Baxter and Stone (1985) reported that, above 3200 m (10,500 ft) in Wyoming, toad tadpoles failed to transform and could be observed at pond margins in September.

They did not know whether the tadpoles overwintered successfully.

On August 30, 1952, an aggregation of recently metamorphosed toads on Alum Creek in Hayden Valley in Yellowstone intrigued Turner (1952). Apparently, the newly transformed toads gathered together in large masses about 3 m (yd) from surface water. But after three days, most of the toads had died, apparently from desiccation. Why they did not move a short distance to available surface water remained a mystery to Turner.

Boreal Chorus Frog
Pseudacris triseriata maculata

Adult boreal chorus frogs are distinguished from other adult amphibians in the region by their small size, small toe discs, or pads, on the ends of the toes, relative lack of webbing on the hind feet, and the characteristic three stripes (which are sometimes incomplete) running down the back. Young, small spotted frogs can sometimes be confused with chorus frog adults, but they lack the toe discs, the three stripes, and have longer legs and more-webbed hind feet. A member of the tree frog family, chorus frogs use their toe discs to help them climb short distances up into vegetation. The cover photograph for this book shows the male of this species calling in springtime to attract a mate. Chorus frogs are common and widespread throughout both parks.

Boreal chorus frogs are members of the tree frog family (Hylidae), and are the only members of this family found in either national park. Most species of tree frogs, including this subspecies, are small, have well-developed pads on the tips of their toes, and an extra cartilaginous segment ("intercalary cartilage") between the last two elements of each toe. Chorus frogs are the only common species of amphibian in Yellowstone or Grand Teton National Park that have a loud, clearly identifiable, and commonly heard call.

Description

ADULTS.   Adult boreal chorus frogs are small, usually not exceeding 4 cm (1.5 in.) in length in this region. Females attain a larger size than males. Chorus frogs have a pointed snout, slender body, relatively short legs, and minimal webbing on their hind feet. Their toe pads are small, and their skin is relatively smooth. We most commonly observed individuals with a tan base color (less commonly light green). Three dark stripes run the length of the animal's back. These three stripes give the Latin "specific" name *triseriata* to this frog. These stripes may be somewhat incomplete or broken down the length of the back of some individuals, but the appearance of stripes remains. Two additional lateral stripes pass along each side of the animal and through the face and eye, giving the frog a "masked" appearance. Males have darker throats than females. Boreal chorus frogs have the ability to lighten or darken their color. Carpenter (1953a) observed that the two main color phases—tan and green—occurred in the same population, and there was no intergradation of colors. All frogs were either brown (tan) or green. We have observed the green color phase south of Yellowstone Lake and in the Tetons.

Of the 415 boreal chorus frogs captured in live traps at Ice Lake Reservoir in Yellowstone in 1993, 381 individuals were partly or mostly green (Steven Hill, Montana State University, personal communication, 1994). Also, all 415 animals had light-colored throats, as opposed to the darker throats typical of mature males of the species. The male boreal chorus frogs heard calling in the meadow adjacent to Ice Lake were the brown color phase more typically seen in other parts of the region. Part of the peak of 34 chorus frogs captured on August 8 may have been individuals moving to Ice Lake from breeding sites in the surrounding wet meadows; they had recently metamorphosed from larvae into adults.

TADPOLES.   Boreal chorus frog tadpoles generally do not exceed 3 cm (1.25 in.) in length (Nussbaum et al. 1983), and appear to us to be lightest in color of the three commonest species of amphibians in both parks that have tadpoles (the other two species being boreal toads and spotted frogs). The lighter appearance may be attributable to the bright flecking lying against a brown base color above and cream color below. The eyes of this tadpole are situated farther on the side of the head than the eyes of the other two species mentioned above. Their eyes can be seen projecting beyond the margin of the body when viewed from directly above.

SIMILAR SPECIES.   Young spotted frogs are the only frogs that might be confused with chorus frogs. Spotted frogs lack stripes, lack toe pads, have dorsolateral folds (glandular ridges extending along both sides of the back), and have heavier bodies, longer legs, and more webbing on the hind feet.

Distribution

The range of the boreal chorus frog extends along the Rocky Mountains and the northern plains of North America, from western Alberta, Canada, central Idaho, and central Utah east to central Ontario, Canada, Minnesota and Nebraska, and southward through Colorado into parts of Arizona and New Mexico (Stebbins 1985). This frog is ubiquitous in the Greater Yellowstone Ecosystem and seems to be almost anywhere standing water can be found in the springtime. We have observed chorus frogs at elevations as high as 2865 m (9400 ft) at Togwotee Pass, east of Jackson Hole, and as low as 1600 m (5280 ft) near the Yellowstone River where it leaves Yellowstone Park. Outside the Greater Yellowstone Eco-

The most common color phase we have seen of the chorus frog in the region is a tan base color. However, we have also observed the green coloration in chorus frog adults, like this one, in several places. Other characteristics for identifying this species remain the same as in the tan color phase.

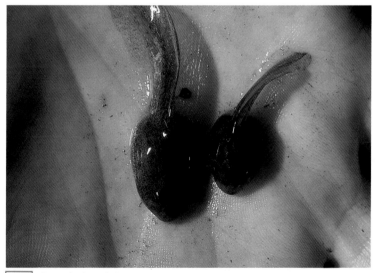

The tadpoles of the chorus frog and the spotted frog are perhaps the most difficult to tell apart of all life stages of all species of amphibians or reptiles commonly found in the region. On the left in this photograph is the larger spotted frog tadpole, and on the right is the smaller chorus frog tadpole. Notice the position of the eyes on the body of each tadpole when viewed from above; eyes of the spotted frog tadpole are well within the body margin, whereas the chorus frog tadpole's eyes are placed laterally, near the edge of the body margin. Both species have a brown base color, but chorus frog tadpoles often have gold-colored "flecks" on their bodies.

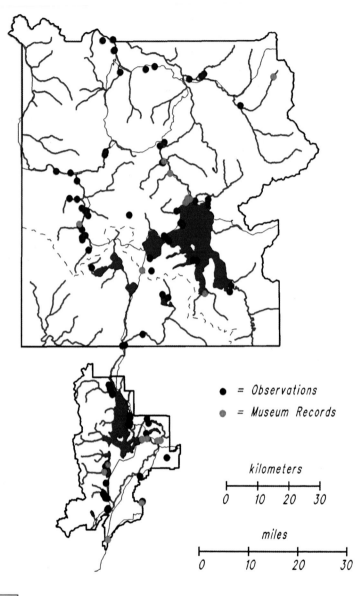

• = *Observations*

• = *Museum Records*

kilometers

0   10   20   30

miles

0   10   20   30

Boreal chorus frogs occur in a variety of locations from the warm, arid northern range of Yellowstone to the cool mountain wetlands of the Tetons to the south. Despite the ease with which calling males can be detected during the spring breeding season, many places in both parks remain unsampled.

system it is found throughout Wyoming (Baxter and Stone 1985), in central and eastern Montana (Stebbins 1985), and parts of southern Idaho (Nussbaum et al. 1983).

ABUNDANCE/STATUS.   On the basis of the number of individuals we have heard calling in the spring, we consider this species to be common to abundant in the Greater Yellowstone Ecosystem. After the adults leave the breeding ponds, however, they are difficult to find. Turner (1955) stated: "This little chorus frog is one of the commonest amphibians of Yellowstone Park, but due to its small size and secretive habits it is rarely observed." Carpenter (1953a) admitted that, after careful observation, he found the chorus frog to be more abundant in the Jackson Hole area than he had originally suspected. We have observed thousands of recently transformed chorus frogs along the south shore of the main portion of Yellowstone Lake, west of the South Arm.

Natural History

HABITAT.   Boreal chorus frogs are believed to hibernate underground, often in burrows made by other animal species. After emergence they move to breeding sites that include marshes, lakes, beaver ponds, vernal ponds, and almost any shallow water with emergent vegetation to which the eggs can be attached. In 1993 at Ice Lake Reservoir in Yellowstone, boreal chorus frogs called from small pools of water in wet meadow habitat adjacent to the lake, but never from the lake itself (Steven Hill, personal communication, 1993), indicating that the preferred breeding sites may have been in the wet meadow rather than in the permanent, deeper body of water. This preference was true despite the fact that some emergent vegetation existed along the shore of the lake itself for eggs to be attached to. After the breeding season, adult boreal chorus frogs are most likely to be encountered in wet meadows or in grass along streams. The boreal chorus frog apparently spends little time off the ground on and in vegetation, as opposed to some of the more arboreal members of the tree frog family. In August 1989 we had the good fortune to observe several dozen adult chorus frogs apparently foraging in meadow habitat adjacent to the Yellowstone River, 3 km (2 mi) upstream from the South-

Chorus frogs are common at Taggart Lake in Grand Teton National Park, one of several sites where we monitor amphibian population trends. Typically, chorus frogs will not be found in deep, open water, but instead in the springtime occur in flooded meadows and areas with plentiful emergent vegetation. In summer, adults spend time foraging in adjacent meadow habitats, using animal burrows to escape heat and dryness. We have also found spotted frogs, tiger salamanders, and wandering garter snakes at this site.

east Arm of Yellowstone Lake. We located them on a cloudy day in grasses 50 cm (1.5 ft) tall along embankments of an old slough, or river channel, with little surface water apparent in the area. The ground, however, was damp, and the humidity was high. Both the brown and green color phases were observed at this site. Of the 48 aquatic sites Hill and Moore (1994) examined on Yellowstone's northern range in 1992 and 1993, the 19 sites where boreal chorus frogs were present had a significantly higher percentage of emergent vegetation (average 84%) than sites without chorus frogs (average 66%).

ACTIVITY PATTERNS.   Adult chorus frogs emerge from hibernation sites in the springtime and gather at breeding sites. Calling may begin as early as April in some parts of the region and may extend into early July at higher elevations. Through the use of automated tape recordings, we have found that the calling activity of chorus frogs in nearby southeastern Idaho is highest between sunset and 2:00 a.m., although calling also occurs during the day. Because of the difficulty in observing chorus frogs after they leave the breeding sites, we do not have extensive information on their daily activity patterns. However, some information is available for this species at Ice Lake Reservoir in Yellowstone near Gardiner, Montana. A total of 415 boreal chorus frogs were captured in live traps in a meadow adjacent to Ice Lake Reservoir, for the first time in 1993 on June 1, and ending on October 10 (Steven Hill, personal communication, 1994). The vast majority of chorus frogs captured throughout 1993 were between July 20 and September 16, with a peak of 34 individuals captured on August 8.

FEEDING HABITS.   Adult boreal chorus frogs are reported to eat ants, spiders, flies, beetles, aphids, and other insects (Campbell 1970, Nussbaum et al. 1983). Tadpoles probably eat vegetation and filter sediments from the bottom of ponds. In the Tetons, aquatic snails may be a competitor with boreal chorus frog tadpoles, reducing growth rate and survival of tadpoles in ponds where snail abundance is high (Woodward and Mitchell 1992).

ENEMIES/DEFENSE.   Potential predators are likely very numerous and include predaceous insects, fish, garter snakes, mammals such as badgers, and several species of birds. We have observed garter snakes eating newly metamorphosed chorus frogs at a site at a pond east of the South Entrance to Yellowstone. In August 1989, we observed a pair of ravens land at the edge of a wetland area near the shore of Yellowstone Lake and behave as if they were capturing chorus frogs in the water where we had observed the frogs moments before. In the Tetons, larval tiger salamanders preyed heavily on smaller (5–8.5 mm [about 0.25 in.] long) chorus frog tadpoles, as did predaceous beetles and insect larvae (Woodward and Mitchell 1992).

REPRODUCTION/DEVELOPMENT.   It is the male of this species that calls vociferously from breeding pools in the springtime, almost to the exclusion of most other sounds in the area. The call of this

Chorus frog males call from shallow water breeding sites in springtime, and are commonly heard by many park visitors. Females visit males at these sites, and lay about 20 eggs at a time on stalks of vegetation, as in this photograph taken at a pond near Togwotee Pass, east of Grand Teton National Park. Like most other life stages of this species, egg masses can be very hard to find.

frog sounds much like the sound of fingers dragged along the teeth of a hard plastic comb. We have observed that each call lasts about 1 second, and a frog may call as frequently as 10 to 20 times per minute. The rate of calling and the frequency of pulses within each call probably depend on temperature (Platz 1989). When a male calls, its throat expands enormously, nearly doubling the size of the animal. The voice of an individual can be heard for hundreds of meters (yards). It takes a tremendous amount of energy for frogs to produce these sounds. For example, when gray tree frogs (*Hyla versicolor*) call, they may raise their metabolic rate by more than 15 times over resting levels (Taigen and Wells 1985).

With patience and persistence, the careful observer can witness and even photograph this marvelous behavior at close range. The best time to do so is at night, when calling is most frequent and frogs seem most secure with being active. With rubber boots, a flashlight, and possibly a tape recorder and a camera with a flash, slowly enter a shallow, marshy area where frogs are calling. It helps tremendously to have more than one person so you can locate a calling frog by "triangulation." However, one person can do this simply by listening and getting a bearing at one point, then changing positions to listen and gain a second bearing. Once the general area has been identified, the observer can gently enter the area, get comfortable, and stand (or sit on an overturned bucket) perfectly still for *several minutes* in the dark. One hopes that the call of distant frogs will filter back to your area, stimulating the frogs around you to resume calling. Or, if you have a recording of the frog's call, playing the recording can elicit responses from frogs nearby. Chorus frogs will eventually begin calling on their own without any stimulation if the observer remains very patient and very still.

Once these frogs are calling, the observer can slowly allow the beam of the flashlight to shine around them, looking carefully at the base of shoots of vegetation and floating sticks for calling frogs. The first frog will be the most difficult to find, but once you know what you are looking for and a "search image" has formed in your mind, it will become easier to see these diminutive frogs. If you are lucky, and in an area of high frog density, you will be able to see several males with their throat pouches expanding and contracting, and you will likely be amazed at just how loud such a small animal can be. We have even been able to make these observations during the day in some areas.

Female chorus frogs can produce from 150 to 1500 eggs, and they lay them in separate packets of eggs with 30 to 75 eggs each (Nussbaum et al. 1983). Eggs will generally hatch in 10 to 14 days, depending on temperature. We have observed only about 20 or so eggs per egg mass in Yellowstone and at Togwotee Pass, east of Jackson Hole. Each egg mass is firmly attached to a stalk of vegetation, from 5 to 12 cm (2 to 5 in.) below the surface of the water. Like other life stages of this animal, their eggs masses are not very conspicuous.

After hatching, chorus frog tadpoles probably spend time in shallow water areas with emergent vegetation. We observed many thousands of recently metamorphosed chorus frogs along the south shore of the main portion of Yellowstone Lake, east of West

Thumb, during the third week of August 1989. They were found along the margins of standing pools of water, which were isolated from the lake itself by large gravel bars. We also observed adults adjacent to the lake in similar habitats with emergent vegetation.

Spotted Frog
Rana pretiosa

Adult spotted frogs may be the most commonly observed of the region's herpetofauna because they are common and widespread in both parks and because they frequently leap from a grassy streambank into nearby water for refuge with a loud "kerplunk" as a person passes by. Adult spotted frogs have large, fully webbed hind feet, pointed snout, skin with black spots that are sometimes raised, and salmon-colored underside (see next photo). Small spotted frogs can look similar to chorus frogs, but upon further inspection of the identifying features, these two species can be differentiated.

Spotted frogs are one of three species of frogs occurring in the Greater Yellowstone Ecosystem that belong to the true frog family (Ranidae). Recent studies of the genetics of spotted frogs indicate that what we refer to today as the spotted frog may actually be more than one species (David Green, Redpath Museum, McGill University, personal communication, 1991). Some populations on the periphery of the range appear to have diverged sufficiently to warrant classifying them as new species. The spotted frogs found in Yellowstone and Grand Teton National Parks may not retain their current name of *Rana pretiosa*.

Description

ADULTS. Spotted frogs are medium sized, with adults reaching body lengths of up to 9 cm (3.5 in.) (Turner 1955), although they are usually smaller. Female spotted frogs attain larger sizes than males. The snout is somewhat pointed, and the eyes are oriented upward and outward. Mature males have thicker thumbs than females, with a dark, roughened area called a *nuptial pad* during the breeding season. These pads presumably aid the male in holding onto the female during amplexus (the mating position). The rear feet are relatively large for the frog, and the long hind toes are nearly fully webbed. Spotted frogs are generally green or brownish green with black spots on the back and a somewhat bumpy or "warty" texture to the skin. In this region, we have observed only the salmon-red coloration on the underside of the legs and belly, but in other regions where this species occurs, the underside may be yellow.

TADPOLES. Shortly after hatching, tadpoles are dark and about 1.2 cm (0.5 in.) in length, with the tail composing 75% of the length of the animal (Turner 1958a). By the time the tadpole is ready to metamorphose into an adult, it may be brownish green, speckled

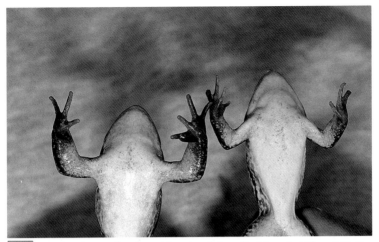

The thumb size of male and female adult spotted frogs is different. Notice the swollen appearance of the thumbs of the male spotted frog, at right in this photograph, compared to the female at left. Males will hook their thumbs around the female's torso during breeding in a position called amplexus.

An easy way to tell spotted frogs from all other amphibian species in the region is to examine its ventral side along its belly and legs for a salmon-red coloration, such as in this photograph. Also note the size of the feet and length and thickness of the legs. Spotted frogs are much better leapers than boreal toads, and their body shape sometimes indicates that. Young spotted frogs may have little or no salmon coloration underneath.

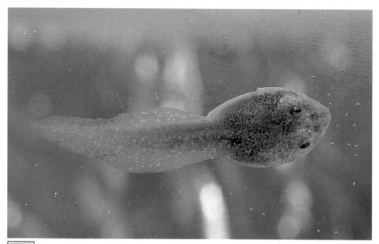

Spotted frog tadpoles have a brown base color, and are very similar in appearance to chorus frog tadpoles (see comparison photograph in the section on chorus frogs). A key distinguishing characteristic is the placement of the eyes of spotted frog tadpoles close together, nearer the body midline (not far apart toward the body margin as with chorus frogs).

with light flecks. It will have four legs and may be as long as 6 cm (2.5 in.), with the tail composing about 66% of that length.

SIMILAR SPECIES.   Large adult spotted frogs might be confused with the boreal toad because of the bumps on their skin. But the greenish hue of the frog, the webbed hind feet, more pointed snout, and the salmon-red color underneath, all distinguish this species from the toad, which is usually tan with a white stripe down the back. The action of the frog leaping into water from a grassy bank with a loud "kerplunk" in the Greater Yellowstone Ecosystem is the tell-tale sign of a spotted frog heading for cover.

Young spotted frogs 3 cm (1.25 in.) in length or less may be difficult to distinguish from the boreal chorus frog. Remember that the juvenile spotted frog looks much like the adult, but without much red coloration underneath, if any, whereas the boreal chorus frog is lighter in color (closer to tan or lime green) with darker brown stripes running the length of the back and sides, and few or no black spots. The northern leopard frog is similar in appearance to the spotted frog, except it has a lighter green base color; larger, more regularly spaced black spots with light borders; and no raised bumps. Most importantly, northern leopard frogs have not been seen in this region for 40 years, and even then only in String, Jenny, and Beaver Dick Lakes. Therefore, the odds of confusing a northern leopard frog for a spotted frog in this region are remote. Bullfrogs are restricted to Kelly Hot Springs in this region and are not found in the same habitats as spotted frogs.

It may be difficult to distinguish tadpoles of this species from the tadpoles of other species found in this region. The eyes of spotted frog tadpoles are located closer to the middle of the animal than the eyes of boreal chorus frog tadpoles, which can be seen to be more laterally positioned, protruding beyond the margin of the head, when viewed from above. Boreal toad tadpoles are darker, rounder, and tend to aggregate more than spotted frog tadpoles. Also, we have observed that spotted frog tadpoles can move much faster to avoid potential predators than can toad tadpoles.

Distribution

The spotted frog ranges from southeast Alaska south through Canada to Oregon and Washington, northern California (historically), northern Nevada, most of Idaho, western Montana, northwestern Wyoming, and discontinuously into northern Utah (Stebbins 1985). The distribution of the spotted frog beyond the Greater Yellowstone Ecosystem continues in the mountains north and west, but drops off south and east of the region. It is widespread in Yellowstone and Grand Teton National Parks.

Abundance/Status

This species is common to abundant throughout Yellowstone and Grand Teton National Parks, but it apparently has declined in the southern and western portions of its range in the United States. It may already be extinct in western Oregon and Washington, and it is almost certainly extinct in northern California (Worthing 1993). Because of these declines, this species is currently classified through most of its range as a C-2 candidate species (meaning that more study is needed) under the federal Endangered Species Act of 1973. It is classified as a C-1 candidate species (meaning that immediate protection is warranted) in the southern and western

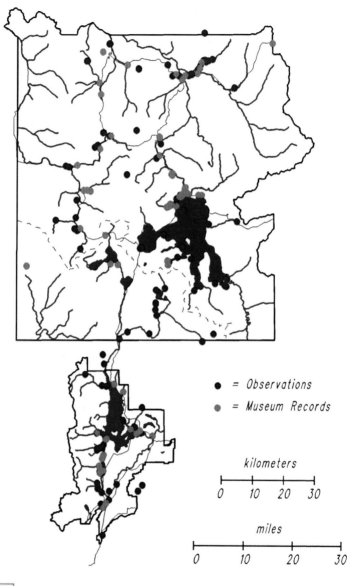

● = Observations

● = Museum Records

kilometers

0   10   20   30

miles

0   10   20   30

Spotted frogs occur in a variety of locations from the warm, arid northern range of Yellowstone to the cool mountain wetlands of the Tetons to the south. Although this species has undergone drastic declines in abundance elsewhere in its range in North America, it appears to remain relatively abundant here. Many places in both parks remain unsampled.

portions of its range. However, because of its abundance in the region covered by this book, its distribution, and its behavior, this species today is probably the most commonly observed species of all the amphibians and reptiles in both parks. If you see a true frog (not a toad or chorus frog) greater than 3 cm (1.25 in.) in length anywhere in either Yellowstone or the Tetons, it will almost always be the spotted frog. The other two species of true frogs discussed in this book—the leopard frog and the bullfrog—are extremely limited in distribution and abundance within the two parks.

Patla and Peterson (1994) have documented an 85% decline in the only population of spotted frogs for which previous population data exist, near Lodge Creek in the lake area in Yellowstone (see following section). However, this decline is probably not from some unknown cause. It is instead more likely a result of construction of a road bisecting habitats used by frogs in the population and of development of a key spring head (where these frogs hibernate) for use as a water supply for the lake area. The good news is that this decline is not likely part of the mysterious decline of amphibian species occurring elsewhere. The bad news is that we have essentially lost one of the best historical population comparison sites known for this species.

Natural History

Most of what is known about the ecology of the spotted frog in Yellowstone National Park is due to the work of Dr. Frederick B. Turner, who conducted studies for his Ph.D. degree on this species at Lodge (previously Soldier) Creek in the Lake Area at the north end of Yellowstone Lake. Consequently, not only do we have extensive, detailed information from natural history studies of this species, but the information was gathered within the region covered by this book. Even though Turner conducted his studies 40 years ago (in the mid-1950s) the research remains today among the best of its kind ever completed. Not only can this be viewed as a testament to Turner's skills as a scientist but also demonstrates that the study of the natural history of frogs has not been widely undertaken. We had the good fortune to have Dr. Turner review his research with us on site during the preparation of this book.

HABITAT. The spotted frog is highly aquatic, almost always closely associated with surface water. It can be found on the banks of almost any pond, lake or stream in the region—even on islands in Yellowstone Lake and Jackson Lake. We most often see this species in wetland sites with emergent vegetation (for example, sedges and grasses). Of the 48 sites surveyed by Hill and Moore in 1992 and 1993 on Yellowstone's northern range, the 22 sites with spotted frogs were significantly deeper (average depth 173 cm [5 ft]) than the 26 sites without spotted frogs (average depth 68 cm [2 ft]) (Hill and Moore 1994).

Adult spotted frogs can migrate from a hibernation site in a permanent body of water (for example, a spring head or stream) to a breeding pond, then to a wetland or creek for the summer months, and then back to the hibernation site. At certain times of year, frogs may move so frequently, and for dozens and even hundreds of meters (yards) in distance, that it is impractical to identify a "home range" for a given individual (Turner 1960). Alternatively, spotted frogs may hibernate, breed, and spend the active season all in the same area of a permanent body of water.

ACTIVITY PATTERNS. Spotted frogs emerge from hibernation in the Yellowstone Lake area beginning in May (Turner 1958a). Spotted frogs were observed on April 10, 1926, in Biscuit Basin after a period of warm weather but had not appeared a week later in the Old Faithful area (Yeager 1926). Spotted frogs are primarily diurnal with peak activity occurring about midday (Turner 1960). Adult spotted frogs seem to be most active when water temperatures are between 10 and 26°C (50 and 79°F).

Spotted frogs in the Yellowstone Lake area may live to be 10 years of age or older (Turner 1960). This longevity contrasts sharply with that of spotted frogs from coastal British Columbia, Canada, where the average individual may not live past 3 years of age (Licht 1975). Also, the same amount of growth British Columbia frogs achieve in 2 to 3 years takes Yellowstone frogs 8 to 10 years. This difference is probably related to the length of the growing season available to spotted frogs in each locality. British Columbia frogs are active from February through October, whereas Yellowstone frogs are active primarily from late May to Septem-

At Lodge Creek, near the Yellowstone Lake Lodge, one of the most well-known studies of spotted frogs took place over 40 years ago. We continue to use this site today to monitor amphibian populations. Unlike at sites with a permanent body of standing water (e.g., Slide Lake), adults here breed in separate, temporary pools in springtime, and migrate to permanent streams such as this in the summer months before returning to a spring head to hibernate for the winter. We have also found chorus frogs, boreal toads, and wandering garter snakes near this site.

Spotted frogs are common at Slide Lake, an amphibian monitoring site in the northern portion of Yellowstone near Mammoth, Wyoming. As at most breeding sites, spotted frogs lay their egg masses on the north (i.e., south-facing) shore to take maximum advantage of the sun. Adults can be found all around the lakeshore in summertime and do not need to make seasonal migrations to other water bodies, as they do at the Lodge Creek site. We have also found chorus frogs, tiger salamanders, and wandering garter snakes at this site.

ber. Spotted frogs in Yellowstone probably don't even breed before 3 years of age, after the age at which spotted frogs in coastal British Columbia would already have died.

FEEDING HABITS.   Adult spotted frogs eat mostly insects and feed almost exclusively during the day or at dusk (Turner 1959). Turner (1959) suggested that timing of feeding may simply be related to prey availability—insects may be less active at night in this region. In early summer, frogs do not range as far for food items as they do later in the season, and July and August are the months when frogs eat the most. Food items include spiders, ants, beetles, moths, dragonflies, mayflies, caddisflies, snails, mosquitos, worms, grasshoppers, crickets, and whatever else the frogs can find (Turner 1959).

ENEMIES/DEFENSE.   The sheer abundance of spotted frogs provides an important source of protein to the region's predators, and many animals feed on them, including herons, egrets, sandhill cranes, ravens, and otters. We have found spotted frog tadpoles, juveniles, and adults in the stomachs of wandering garter snakes. We have received reports of great gray owls capturing spotted frogs near Fishing Bridge, and we once found a recently eaten frog in the stomach of a trout in Yellowstone. No doubt some of the region's more adaptable predators, such as badgers, coyotes and bears, also eat spotted frogs.

Carpenter (1953a) noted parasites—namely, leeches—on spotted frogs in the Jackson Hole area. Turner (1958b) observed that older spotted frogs hosted in their body cavity significantly more helminth parasites of various species than younger frogs.

REPRODUCTION/DEVELOPMENT.   Male spotted frogs call, albeit faintly, to attract females. Turner (1958a) described their calling as follows:

> While breeding is in progress, males may call weakly from the edges of the ponds, usually at night but occasionally by day. The call is a series of bursts of 4 to 30 or more short croaks occurring at a rate of 3 or 4 per second with individual bursts separated by about 3 seconds. Calling is sporadic, several min-

utes elapsing between calls, or two or more males may call simultaneously. The call is so faint that if [chorus frogs are] calling at the same pond the calls of the spotted frog are nearly
inaudible. When no [chorus frogs] were present I found the distance at which I could just hear the calls was about [25 m] 80 ft.

Males begin breeding in their fourth year (Turner 1960) and
usually outnumber females at the breeding ponds, apparently because they stay there longer than females (Turner 1958a). Females
begin breeding in their fifth or sixth year. Older female frogs were
3.5 times more abundant than similar-aged male spotted frogs in
the Yellowstone Lake area (Turner 1960). They may move to the
breeding ponds, lay their eggs, and leave, while males stay to try
to continue breeding. Males can breed in two or three successive
years, but females apparently cannot breed more frequently than
every other year; the energetic requirements of developing eggs
every year may be too great in this region, considering the relatively short season in which frogs can be active. A male frog grasps
a female around the waist, in a position called *amplexus,* and fer-
tilizes eggs as the female extrudes them.

Egg deposition begins in the Yellowstone Lake area in May and
may continue into early June (Turner 1958a). Eggs are laid on the
bottom of the pond and swell to a softball-sized mass of from 150
to 500 cubic centimeters floating just under the surface of the water at sites with no current, or flow, usually on the north (that is,
south-facing) shore in full sunlight. An egg mass contains from
200 to 800 eggs per mass, and eggs average 11 mm in diameter.
Eggs swell when they contact the water as they are extruded by
the female, creating the large mass, which looks like clear gelatin
with little black flecks clearly visible in the middle of each egg.
We observed an egg mass in Indian Pond near the Lake Area in
Yellowstone in May that was laid in a geothermally influenced
area. The eggs were at about 23°C (76°F), and the range of temperatures available nearby was from 15 to 35°C (59 to 95°F).

Many females may deposit their egg masses at the same site.
We observed 34 separate egg masses together at one site in the
Tetons and about 45 egg masses together at a site in Upper Red
Rocks Lake in Montana, west of West Yellowstone. Apparently,

The conspicuous egg masses of the spotted frog are easily distinguishable from egg masses of other species. These frogs lay eggs on the muddy bottom at shallow wetland sites. The softball-sized egg mass soon floats to the water surface, and begins to accumulate algae and debris. Water temperatures within each egg mass can be significantly higher than water temperatures outside the egg mass, thus speeding incubation of the eggs.

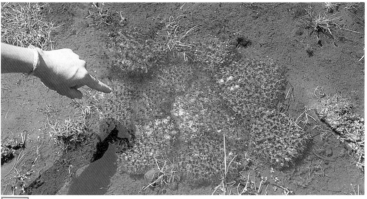

We often find several spotted frog egg masses togeth- at one location, such as this group at Taggart Lake in the Tetons. In t   tuation, not only are water temperatures warmer within each egg mas   t water temperatures are warmer outside each egg mass in the mic   of the group of masses than in surrounding water.

As spotted frog tadpoles transform into adults, they grow hind legs first, then the left front leg, and finally the right front leg. The tail remains for a while as the animal learns to hop about on land.

population size of breeding females may be estimated based on the number of egg masses observed (Corn and Livo 1989).

We have observed that an individual egg mass appears to be adapted to collect and hold heat, and temperatures in the middle of an egg mass may be several degrees warmer than water temperatures outside the egg mass. Egg masses may be attached to rooted vegetation or they may float free and may even be blown about by the wind. Freshly laid egg masses will be mostly clear, whereas older egg masses will be green from an algae growing in and around the egg mass. Egg masses can also accumulate debris on the surface and sides.

Tadpoles may emerge from 12 to 21 days after egg deposition (Turner 1958a), depending on temperature. Eggs hatched in the Yellowstone Lake area as early as June 4 in 1954 and as late as June 30 in 1955 (Turner 1958a). Tadpoles usually have hind legs by 40 to 50 days after hatching, and front legs follow; the left front leg grows in first with the right front leg following shortly thereafter. Tadpoles gather together in large aggregations near where they hatched, perhaps to maximize heat gain or forage more efficiently (Carpenter 1953b).

Tadpoles have several rows of labial "teeth" or horny ridges on their lips. They use these "teeth" to eat, scraping algae and vegetation off rocks and other surfaces found in the breeding ponds. For a period of 10 to 15 days before an individual tadpole metamorphoses into an adult, the individual grows larger, with better developed legs, and basks at the edge of the pond. The tadpole's tail, which not only propels it through the water but also stores energy, begins to shrink as the animal approaches the time of transformation into the adult stage. After transformation, individuals may remain at the edge of the pond for several days before migrating from breeding pools to permanent bodies of water, if they are separate, or spreading out to new territory on the same body of water from which they hatched. Survival to metamorphosis in some years can be almost zero due to deaths from drought or freezing, but in warmer, wetter years, survival can be significant (Turner 1960).

Northern Leopard Frog

Rana pipiens

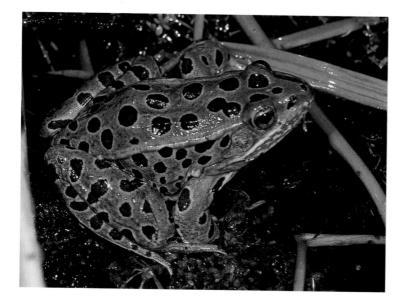

Adult leopard frogs are distinguished from spotted frogs by their lighter ground color (usually green but sometimes brown) and large, round black spots with a lighter "halo" around each spot. In this region, the leopard frog was found along String and Jenny Lakes in Jackson Hole (now Grand Teton National Park). However, this species has not been observed in 40 years, and we believe it is extinct here.

We will not discuss in detail the northern leopard frog because the likelihood of encountering this species in the region covered by this book is extremely low. However, any observations made of this species are extremely valuable, so if you do see one, please report it. Like the spotted frog, the northern leopard frog is a member of the family of true frogs (Ranidae).

Description
Northern leopard frogs may grow to 10 cm (4 in.) in length (Nussbaum et al. 1983). They have a green (and sometimes brown) ground color, which generally is lighter than that of the spotted frog, and they are uniformly white underneath. These frogs have many large, regularly spaced black spots on their backs and sides, with light borders around each spot. The prominent spots give a leopardlike appearance to the skin of the northern leopard frog. Its skin does not have the "warty" texture of large adult spotted frogs.

Distribution
The northern leopard frog is perhaps the most widely distributed amphibian in the United States, found everywhere except the west coast of North America and the extreme southeast (Stebbins 1985). Although it is not confirmed to have occurred in Yellowstone National Park, it historically occurred in Jackson Hole. Collections have been made of the northern leopard frog in Jenny, String, and Beaver Dick Lakes, south of Jackson Lake against the base of the Teton Range. Carpenter (1953a) reported that leopard frogs were common along the grass-sedge shores of String Lake. However, nearly 40 years have passed since the last known observation or collection of a northern leopard frog was recorded.

Turner (1955) stated: "The occurrence of this frog has been reported by Tanner (1931) along the Madison River near the west entrance to Yellowstone Park. Apparently, the populations are neither large nor extensive." Turner (University of California, Los

The wetlands along the west shore of String Lake are the last known locations where leopard frogs occurred. We and others have searched here several times to find leopard frogs without success.

Angeles, personal communication, 1989) later confided that he was uncertain of the validity of this record. Northern leopard frogs do occur downstream from this site in Montana in the Madison/ Missouri River drainage (Thompson 1982).

We received a report of a northern leopard frog in the large meadows of the Bechler region of Yellowstone in 1992. Also, northern leopard frogs have been collected in the past from the Targhee National Forest just west of the boundary to Yellowstone National Park. But, just as in Jackson Hole, the northern leopard frog has not been documented as existing on the Targhee Forest since 1950 (Clark et al. 1993, Clark and Peterson 1994). A fair amount of effort has been expended recently by several individuals, including us, to find leopard frogs in the Tetons and on the Targhee Forest, but to no avail. We hope that some of you who read this book will also try to find this species in these areas. We also hope that you document your efforts carefully and report them (see chapter "Information Needs: How You Can Contribute").

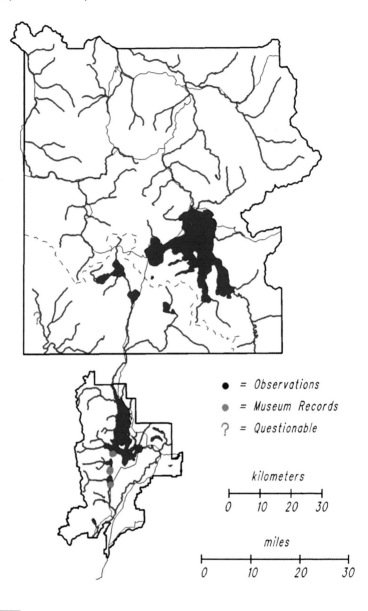

● = Observations
● = Museum Records
? = Questionable

kilometers

0   10   20   30

miles

0   10   20   30

Leopard frogs occurred only in Jenny, String, and Leigh Lakes in Grand Teton National Park. However, they have remained undetected over the last 40 years, despite repeated searches to find them. We suspect they may be extinct here, but only repeated searches in this area might confirm this.

Because of the wide distribution of this species in North America and the fact that it is found nearby downstream in the Snake River drainage (Nussbaum et al. 1983, Baxter and Stone 1985), we suspect the northern leopard frog was native to Jackson Hole area and the Targhee Forest and was not introduced.

Abundance/Status
The northern leopard frog is seriously declining and becoming locally extinct in parts of its range in the United States. In Colorado and eastern Wyoming, the leopard frog has disappeared from nearly 85% of sites where it occurred historically (Corn et al. 1989). Most disturbing is the fact that in some areas such as Rocky Mountain National Park in Colorado, as well as in the Greater Yellowstone Ecosystem, natural wetland habitat remains apparently undisturbed with acceptable water quality, but the frogs are gone. The northern leopard frog appears to be extinct in the region covered by this book.

Natural History
We know very little about the northern leopard frog in this region, although more is known about this species in general (from other regions) than for most other species of amphibians. For more information on this species in the northwestern United States, see Nussbaum et al. (1983) and Baxter and Stone (1985).

Bullfrog
Rana catesbeiana

The bullfrog grows much larger than spotted frogs and is found only where it was introduced, in and near Kelly Warm Springs in Jackson Hole, just outside Grand Teton National Park. Its generally green color, ridge over the tympanum (or ear, behind the eye on the side of the head) and large size are distinctive. It is a highly aquatic species of frog and can leap far and swim rapidly. In many places where bullfrogs have been introduced, native wildlife populations have suffered from predation and competition.

Bullfrogs are members of the true frog family (Ranidae). The name indicates their loud, bellowing call. Because they are not native to the Greater Yellowstone Ecosystem, and they are extremely limited in their distribution in the region, we do not provide much information concerning their ecology.

Description

ADULTS. Bullfrogs grow to large sizes – over 150 mm (6 in.) in length. They are mostly olive green or brown, with brighter green alongside the head and white underneath.

TADPOLES. Tadpoles less than 25 mm (1 in.) in length appear black with transverse gold bands on the head and body. Tadpoles can grow to 110 mm (4.5 in.) in length and are olive green on top with many small black spots, and cream-colored underneath (Nussbaum et al. 1983).

Distribution

The bullfrog is an introduced species in this region. It historically occurred east of the continental divide from southern Canada to Mexico (Stebbins 1985). It has been widely introduced in the western United States. In this region, we know it to occur only in Kelly Warm Springs and its outflow in Grand Teton National Park and possibly at another warm spring on the south side of the nearby Gros Ventre River. At the high elevations found in these two national parks, the bullfrog probably could not survive and reproduce outside of geothermally heated waters. At Kelly Warm Springs, however, this species is successfully reproducing; we have observed egg masses and tadpoles there. Males have even been heard calling in the middle of the winter (Steve Beaupre, University of Pennsylvania, personal communication, 1993).

Abundance/Status
Bullfrogs are common at Kelly Warm Springs.

Natural History
The highly aquatic bullfrog is a large, aggressive animal and a formidable predator. Bullfrogs are sometimes responsible for causing local extinctions of native amphibians where they are introduced (Hayes and Jennings 1986). Other native animals, especially desert fishes, can suffer losses when exotic species such as the bullfrog are introduced into their environment (Miller and Hubbs 1960, Williams and Sada 1985). Remember, it is usually a bad idea to introduce a non-native animal into a new environment. In Yellowstone and the Tetons, hot springs are sources of unique forms of aquatic life and plant and animal communities that are highly sensitive. Exotic species such as bullfrogs could permanently and irreversibly alter these communities. For more information on bullfrogs in the northwestern United States, see Nussbaum et al. (1983) and Baxter and Stone (1985).

Reptiles
Species Accounts

THE CLASS OF vertebrates known as the Reptilia is made up of a diverse group of animals including turtles, crocodiles, lizards, snakes, and the tuatara of New Zealand. The word "reptile" is based on the Latin word meaning to crawl. The tuatara, lizards, and snakes are relatively closely related to each other; turtles and crocodilians are more distantly related. In fact, crocodiles are more closely related to the dinosaurs and birds than to other groups of reptiles. These different groups are classified together, however, because they share a number of functional characteristics. Most reptiles have a dry, scaly skin. Contrary to popular belief, reptiles (including snakes) are not slimy or even moist. Their skin helps reduce water loss so they can survive even in very dry conditions (for example, deserts). Reptiles periodically shed their skins, either in pieces (as in most lizards) or in a single piece (as in snakes). All reptiles breathe through lungs, and most cannot exchange gases across their skin to the extent amphibians do.

Reptiles are nearly always ectothermic. This term means that they derive their body heat primarily from an outside source such as the sun or the ground. Although their body temperatures are limited by the range of temperatures that occurs in their environment, most reptiles are adept at regulating their body temperature through their behavior by selecting when and where they will be active. For example, on a warm, sunny day, many reptiles can maintain a body temperature within a narrow (1–3°C, or 2–5°F) preferred temperature range for many hours while they forage or move about. The ability of these ectothermic, "cold blooded" animals to maintain relatively constant, warm body temperatures under appropriate conditions by using behavior is similar to the ability endothermic, or "warm blooded," animals have to maintain a similar warm, stable, body temperature through metabolic activity. But endothermic animals maintain this thermal stability by burning much more energy than ectothermic animals.

The activity of ectothermic animals is often limited by low environmental temperatures, especially at night. However, ectothermic animals have the advantage over endothermic animals during times when food is hard to find. When a snake does not need to be active, it may allow its body temperature to cool, thus reducing its metabolic rate considerably and reducing the animal's need to eat. Some snakes can even go for over a year between meals if they have to! Most of the reptiles in the Greater Yellowstone Ecosystem are primarily active during the day because of the very cool temperatures they are faced with at night. The presence of geothermal features undoubtedly has a large effect on the ecology of some of the reptile species that live in the Greater Yellowstone Ecosystem.

All reptiles have internal fertilization and membranes surrounding their embryos similar to those of birds and mammals. Most reptiles have shelled eggs but many bear live young, especially in colder regions like Yellowstone and the Tetons. All reptiles have direct development; there is no larval stage as in amphibians. Usually, juvenile members of a species simply look like miniature versions of the adults. However, the young of some species can have color patterns that are brighter and more distinct than those of the adults.

Most species of reptiles in the world live in the tropics. The number of species of reptiles decreases at higher latitudes (that is, toward the north and south poles). In the United States, the greatest numbers of reptile species occur in the desert southwest, and there are relatively few species of reptiles in the Greater Yellowstone Ecosystem (Kiester 1971). Although the number of species of reptiles that occur in this ecosystem is few, their ecology is

Reptile Elevation Ranges

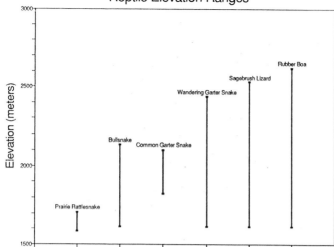

All but one species of reptile, the valley garter snake, are found at the lowest elevation sites in the northern portion of Yellowstone National Park near Gardiner, Montana. Sagebrush lizards, rubber boas, and wandering garter snakes are found up to near 2500 meters (8300 feet) elevation. Rattlesnakes and bull snakes are found only up to near 1700–2100 meters (5600–7000 feet) elevation, respectively. Valley garter snakes enter the region from the southwest and only occur in Jackson Hole and the southwest corner of Yellowstone, near 1800–2100 meters (6000–6900 feet) elevation.

fascinating. A great deal remains to be learned about how these animals survive, grow, and reproduce in an environment that seems so harsh for reptiles.

Six species of reptiles are known to occur in Yellowstone: the northern sagebrush lizard, the rubber boa, the bull snake, the wandering garter snake, the valley garter snake, and the prairie rattlesnake. Four species are confirmed as occurring in the Tetons — all of those listed above except the bull snake and the rattlesnake. The bull snake may occur in the Tetons (where, west of the Continental Divide, it would be a different subspecies called the gopher snake), and the eastern yellowbelly racer snake may occur in Yellowstone. Only one species — the prairie rattlesnake — is highly venomous. However, like most animals, the rattlesnake would like nothing better than to avoid everything (including people) except potential prey or mates.

Northern Sagebrush Lizard
Sceloporus graciosus graciosus

The only lizard known to occur in either park, sagebrush lizards are readily distinguishable from the region's other reptiles which are all snakes. We have heard reports of people confusing salamanders with lizards, but lizards have dry, scaly skin, a more slender appearance, and claws on the ends of the toes. This species can be common where it occurs along the lower Yellowstone River, at one site in the Tetons, and in isolated geothermally influenced areas in various locations in Yellowstone.

The northern sagebrush lizard is the only species of lizard currently known to occur in Yellowstone or Grand Teton National Parks. It is a member of the family Phrynosomatidae.

Description

ADULTS. Because the northern sagebrush lizard is the only lizard species known to occur in the parks, it is rather easily identified. These lizards have a dry skin, keeled (ridged), spiny scales, granular textured scales on the posterior surface of the thighs, four legs, true claws, and a tail. They are relatively small at approximately 13 cm (5 in.) in length from snout to tip of tail, and about 6 cm (2.5 in.) in length from the snout to the vent, which is near the base of the tail (Nussbaum et al. 1983). Mueller (1967) reported that lizards from the Norris Geyser Basin area of Yellowstone Park averaged 4.5 cm (1.8 in.) in length from snout to vent and 3.7 g (0.13 oz) in weight. Dr. Robert Moore (Montana State University, personal communication, 1994) observed that at the Norris area, the lizards with the greatest snout-vent length were females. Males have relatively longer tails and may grow slightly larger than females.

The northern sagebrush lizard is generally gray or light brown, with darker brown stripes on the back set inside lighter stripes on the sides, running the length of the body. The stripes are not always prominent, however, and sometimes form more of a pattern of checks down the back of the animal. These lizards are generally white or cream colored underneath. Males have blue patches on the belly and on each side, with blue mottling on the throat (Baxter and Stone 1985). Sexually mature females may have some pale blue coloration underneath and salmon coloration along their sides and inside of their hind legs (Dr. Robert Moore, personal communication, 1994).

JUVENILES. The young resemble adults, are 29–34 mm at hatching, and grow very slowly in Yellowstone National Park (Mueller and Moore 1969).

SIMILAR SPECIES. The only other species of amphibian or reptile that you might confuse with the lizard in either national park is the blotched tiger salamander, which also has four limbs and a tail. Unlike the lizard, however, the salamander has scaleless, moist skin and no claws on the ends of toes. Also, it is unlikely that you would encounter a tiger salamander in the hotter, drier, rockier habitat of the northern sagebrush lizard.

Distribution
The northern sagebrush lizard is found throughout arid habitats in most of the western United States, from central Washington, southern Idaho, and Montana south to New Mexico, east through Wyoming, and west to California (Stebbins 1985). In the northern Rocky Mountains it is not often found above 1830 m (6000 ft) in elevation (Baxter and Stone 1985). However, in Yellowstone and the Tetons it occurs at higher elevations, up to 2530 m (8300 ft), usually in geothermally influenced areas.

The northern sagebrush lizard has what we consider to be the most interesting distribution pattern of any amphibian or reptile, and perhaps of any animal, in the Greater Yellowstone Ecosystem. Not surprisingly, it is known to occur along the lowest portions of the Yellowstone River in Yellowstone Park near Gardiner, Montana, upstream at least 5 km (3 mi) to the mouth of Bear Creek, so far as we have observed. In this portion of its range it can occur at or below 1830 m (6000 ft) elevation in areas without any geothermal influence. Also found in this region are two other warmth-loving reptiles, the prairie rattlesnake and the bull snake. But the northern sagebrush lizard is also found in many other places throughout Yellowstone National Park, associated with areas that are geothermally influenced and have rocky, subterranean crevices or logs on the ground. Presumably, those populations now limited to areas with geothermal activity were "stranded" during the last few thousand years following a period when the climate changed from warmer than it is now to the cooler climate of the present.

According to what we presently know about these animals, it appears that at high elevations in Yellowstone, populations of these lizards cannot thrive away from areas warmed by heat from

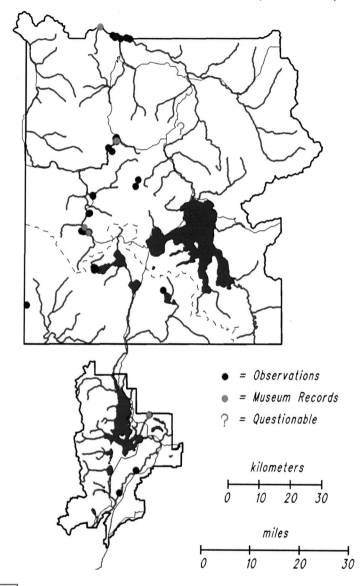

● = Observations

● = Museum Records

? = Questionable

kilometers

0   10   20   30

miles

0   10   20   30

Sagebrush lizards occur along the lower Yellowstone River area, along Pilgrim Creek near the Snake River in the Tetons, and in several geothermally influenced areas at higher elevations in Yellowstone Park. Many places in both parks remain unsampled, so look for sagebrush lizards in lower elevation areas along the Yellowstone and Snake Rivers, and in geothermally influenced areas.

the earth's core. However, our recent observations on the occurrence of the northern sagebrush lizard in the Tetons lead us to conclude that, in at least one area, lizards can exist above 2130 m (7000 ft) in elevation in areas without a geothermal heat source. Populations found in geothermally influenced areas in Yellowstone like Norris Geyser Basin, Shoshone Lake Geyser Basin, Heart Lake Geyser Basin, Gibbon Hill thermal area, Mary Lake thermal area, Boundary Creek thermal area, and several localities along the Firehole River drainage from Old Faithful downstream at least to Porcupine Hill in the Lower Geyser Basin, appear to be isolated from populations outside park boundaries. At some point they may be disjunct from one another within the park, but to what extent we do not know. The degree of separation between populations could be influenced by a number of factors, including whether lizards could find isolated pockets of geothermal refuge between known areas of thermal activity and lizard occurrence.

Lizards may occur elsewhere in both parks than where they are currently known. We have separate reports made at different times from two different people of sagebrush lizards at Washburn Hot Springs on the south side of Mount Washburn at about 2530 m (8300 ft) elevation. Although both observers were credible, they admitted when providing us with the reports that they were not entirely certain of the accuracy of their recollection, so we have represented this location with a question mark on the distribution map. However, because of these two separate reports, we are sufficiently intrigued to place Washburn Hot Springs high on our list of places to look next for lizards in Yellowstone. One other place in Yellowstone from which we received a report is on top of Bunsen Peak near Mammoth Hot Springs, but we are uncertain about the validity of the observation.

Interestingly, the northern sagebrush lizard was not confirmed as occurring in Grand Teton National Park until 1992. Upon searching Grand Teton National Park observation files in the fall of 1991, we found a well-documented observation record for a northern sagebrush lizard near Pilgrim Creek. This observation was reported by two well-known and respected National Park Service biologists, Doug Houston and Glen Cole, on October 2, 1965 (unusually late in the year for lizards to be active). Fortunately, they knew when they saw the lizard that their observation was worth reporting, so they took the time to carefully and thoroughly complete an observation form. However, it was not until August 8, 1992, that we contacted Doug Houston by phone, after we read his observation report and investigated the Pilgrim Creek site in late afternoon (we found no lizards then). After thinking long and hard, Doug was able to verify that the area we had searched, and which we believed was the best potential habitat for lizards along Pilgrim Creek, was indeed the same area where he observed the lizard in 1965. Knowing that our best chance for verifying the occurrence of this species at Pilgrim Creek was to look for them basking in the morning sun, we returned at 9 a.m. on August 9. No more than two minutes after we began searching, we found three northern sagebrush lizards on the surface of a large log. It was only because people took the time to carefully and accurately record their observations that we were able to return 27 years later and verify an extension of the known range of this species in Wyoming by nearly 100 km (60 mi).

Since then we have also received three other observations of the northern sagebrush lizard in the Jackson Hole valley in Grand Teton National Park; two at different locations north of Bar BC Ranch along the gravel hillside on the west side of the Snake River, and one along the Colter Bay Nature Trail. Our knowledge about the hillsides where the observations above the Snake River were made suggests that this area may be suitable lizard habitat, and we would not be surprised to learn that lizards also exist here. We are skeptical about lizards occurring along such a heavily used area as the Colter Bay Nature Trail, however, because it is unlikely that they would have escaped detection for so long. This observation may have been of a salamander. But of course, we cannot be certain until adequate surveys are completed.

It is important to note that the Pilgrim Creek lizard population does *not* appear to benefit from a geothermal heat source, even though they occur at slightly over 2130 m (7000 ft) elevation just inside the border of Grand Teton National Park. Baxter and Stone (1985) noted that this species is found up to 2195 m (7200 ft) elevation in the upper North Platte Valley near Saratoga, Wyoming, in an area without geothermal features. We suspect that even though the Pilgrim Creek population may not depend on a geothermal heat source; it probably benefits from a specific microclimate provided in this area in the gravelly, south-facing slope and may be isolated from the next closest population, wherever that may be.

The distribution of northern sagebrush lizards in Yellowstone was first described in detail by George Algard (1968), a graduate student at Montana State University. He mentioned some of the sites listed above as areas where lizards were then known to occur. Since then, we have been able to build on his original work, to expand the known distribution of northern sagebrush lizards in Yellowstone Park, and to confirm their existence for the first time in Grand Teton National Park. The recent information regarding lizard presence in the Tetons at high elevations outside of geothermally influenced areas and regarding the more widespread distribution in Yellowstone than what was previously believed, leads us to wonder how many additional places in either national park lizards may occur, both within and outside of geothermally influenced areas. The more we have investigated what is known of the distribution of this species, the more their known distribution in the parks has expanded.

Despite the fact that Algard (1968) observed no movement among populations of lizards in the Norris Geyser Basin, we believe it is possible that some populations that we presently assume to be geographically isolated in Yellowstone may not be so. For instance, in the Firehole River Basin so many new areas with lizards have recently been recorded (though the species have probably existed there for long periods of time), it is conceivable that they may not all exist in isolated, disjunct populations strictly associated with individual geothermal features. If lizards can occur in the Tetons above 2130 m (7000 ft) elevation in nongeothermally influenced areas, we cannot rule out the possibility that they may also exist in similar situations in Yellowstone, near or between sites that are obviously geothermally heated. Also, we always presumed that Lizard Creek at the north end of Jackson Lake in Grand Teton National Park was so named because a person saw a salamander there, which reminded him or her of a lizard. Perhaps there is a better reason for the name Lizard Creek.

Abundance/Status

Northern sagebrush lizards may be locally common and relatively easy to observe in the appropriate habitats. Four age classes of lizards are identifiable in the Norris population: juveniles through three years of age (Mueller 1967). Sixty-five percent of growth of individuals occurred in their first year, with growth tapering off dramatically by age three (Mueller and Moore 1969). Algard (1968) calculated a maximum population estimate of 120 individuals in the "Ragged Hills" area on the western side of Norris Geyser Basin, but reasoned that the population may be even larger. Growth of individuals and age of sexual maturity of sagebrush lizards may be affected by the amount of available resources combined with the density of lizards occurring within a population. In southern Utah, individual lizards grew faster and females reproduced at an earlier age during years with greater rainfall (and presumably more food resources) and with reduced densities of lizards in the population (Tinkle et al. 1993).

Natural History

HABITAT. Most interesting about the northern sagebrush lizard in this part of its range is the ability of populations to persist in geothermally influenced areas that presumably would otherwise be too high in elevation. However, do not expect to see these animals right beside your favorite geothermal features, be they geysers or hot springs. These lizards generally occur on the periphery of a geyser basin in rocky hillsides or at the forest edge with logs on the ground. Some portions of the ground are heated, but the area will not be seething with geothermal activity. The only two areas in either national park where northern sagebrush lizards occur outside of geothermally influenced areas — the lower Yellowstone River and Pilgrim Creek in Grand Teton National Park — are comparatively low in elevation and are the warmest and sunniest rocky areas around. These sites benefit from the fact that they have the right combination of factors needed for lizards to exist,

Yellowstone is perhaps most famous for its geysers and other geothermal features. Northern sagebrush lizards often depend on habitats near these sites for survival in an otherwise cool environment. Portions of the Norris Geyser Basin, shown here, harbor a healthy population of sagebrush lizards.

Lizard ecologist Steve Adolph shows where he found sagebrush lizard egg fragments under a log in the Norris Geyser Basin. Lizards do not live in areas seething with geothermal activity. Instead, they survive along the periphery where temperatures are more moderate, and rocks and downed trees provide habitat for individuals to hide, forage, reproduce, and hibernate.

among the most important of which is that they face south, so the
sun warms these areas throughout most of the day.

ACTIVITY PATTERNS.   Northern sagebrush lizards are diurnal, generally observed during warm, sunny weather in dry, rocky habitats, scurrying over open ground within a localized area, then stopping on a perch (crest of a rock or a log) to look for food or potential
predators. Once located, these animals can be fairly easy to observe for extended periods of time, provided the observer does not
disturb them. This situation may be especially true during the
breeding season, when adult males defend territories. You can often see them doing "push-ups" on elevated perches, displaying
their bright blue side patches, warning other males away.

They are moderately active reptiles; they are sometimes called
"swifts," because they can move quickly for short distances. In
the Norris area, sagebrush lizards were active from early May
through mid-September and hibernated for approximately 220
days each year (Mueller 1967, 1969). At 131 days the Norris lizards
have the shortest activity season of 14 populations studied from
Wyoming to California (Tinkle et al. 1993). Remember, though,
that in a nongeothermally influenced site in the Tetons, a lizard
was observed above ground in early October.

Fortunately for those of us interested in the sagebrush lizard in
this region, Charles Mueller (1967) and George Algard (1968) studied this species in Yellowstone while completing their respective
graduate degree programs at Montana State University. Mueller
focused his studies on the Norris Geyser Basin population of sagebrush lizards. He concluded that the constraining feature of the
life history of this species is the time period in which adult lizards
are able to be active. This period is governed by cooler temperatures at higher elevations, but the active period for these lizards
may be extended in geothermally influenced areas. In addition,
evidence now exists to suggest that the ability of lizards to lay
eggs at underground sites with adequately warm temperatures
may govern the ability of some lizards to persist in cold climates
(Porter and Tracy 1983). In geothermally influenced areas in Yellowstone, lizards can find areas to bury eggs with suitable soil

temperatures, and this may play an important role in the ability of the northern sagebrush lizard to successfully reproduce here.

Both Mueller (1967) and Algard (1968) reported a lower than average body temperature of 30.9°C (87°F) for northern sagebrush lizards in Yellowstone's geothermal areas, compared to 35–37°C (95–98°F) for previous studies of lizards of this genus (*Sceloporus*) from other areas. The body temperatures observed were usually higher than either ground temperatures (in most places) or air temperatures, indicating that the lizards basked in the sun or gained heat from isolated patches of geothermally heated ground in the area. Mueller (1967) also found that Yellowstone's northern sagebrush lizards maintain significantly cooler body temperatures in the springtime (28.9°C [85°F]) than in the summertime (32.3°C [90°F]), with intermediate temperatures in the fall.

FEEDING HABITS. Over different portions of their geographic range, northern sagebrush lizards eat beetles, flies, butterflies, moths, caterpillars, ants, wasps, spiders, ticks, mites, aphids, scorpions, and other insects and arthropods (Nussbaum et al. 1983, Baxter and Stone 1985). They are "sit-and-wait" predators rather than active foragers: They will sit for extended periods until a prey item passes by close enough to pursue. This foraging technique presumably requires less energy than if sagebrush lizards actively move about to encounter food.

ENEMIES/DEFENSE. In other regions, several different snake species are known to prey on the northern sagebrush lizard. In the region covered by this book, the predators may include the bull snake, wandering garter snake, and rattlesnake. Also, birds may catch some individuals. Like many lizards, these animals may shed their tail when threatened or actually grabbed. There is a plane of weakness within the vertebrae that determines the point where the tail will break off, and specially designed muscles surround the blood vessels to prevent hemorrhaging (Bellairs and Bryant 1985). The tail will then wiggle by itself for a short period, potentially diverting a predator's attention from the animal and increasing the victim's chance of escape. A new tail will eventually regrow, but often it will have a different appearance than the animal's original tail.

REPRODUCTION/DEVELOPMENT.   Breeding in other parts of their range outside of the region covered by this book generally occurs in early summer, after emergence from hibernation in late spring (Baxter and Stone 1985). Typically, 2 to 7 eggs are then buried in loose soil in June (Algard 1968, Nussbaum et al. 1983). Of 14 sagebrush lizard populations studied from Wyoming to California, lizards from Norris Geyser Basin had the smallest average clutch size at 3.2 eggs per clutch (Tinkle et al. 1993). Juveniles hatch out in middle to late summer after approximately two months of incubation. In the Norris area hatchlings were first observed during the second week in August (Muller 1967, Algard 1968). Northern sagebrush lizards may live for three or more years in Yellowstone (Mueller 1967).

Rubber Boa
Charina bottae

A close relative of the more famous and much larger boas from tropical regions of the world, rubber boas are so named because they look and feel rubbery. Dorsal coloration varies from a uniform brown or olive green color to light tan, with cream coloration underneath. This species is also sometimes called the two-headed snake because the thick tail is similar in appearance to the small head. These animals have been seen in a variety of places in both parks and are probably common where they occur. However, they are so infrequently encountered that we have relatively few observation records for them. In our six years of searching for amphibians and reptiles in the region we have yet to encounter one ourselves. Because rubber boas occur in a wide variety of habitats in this region (and elsewhere), and because of our lack of experience with this species here, we do not provide a photograph of rubber boa habitat (see text).

Rubber boas are members of the relatively primitive snake family Boidae, which includes the boas and pythons that are found primarily in the more tropical parts of the world. Like most snakes of this family, rubber boas have vestigial hind appendages in the form of small bony spurs on either side of the body near the animal's cloaca, or vent. Boas also have two lungs instead of the single lung typical of other, more recently evolved snake families. The rubber boa is one of two species of boas that occur in the United States, and it is the only representative of its family in the Greater Yellowstone Ecosystem.

Description

ADULTS.   Rubber boas are medium-sized snakes, usually ranging in length from 30 to 70 cm (12 to 28 in.) (Nussbaum et al. 1983, Baxter and Stone 1985). Males do not reach lengths as long as those of females but do have relatively longer tails. Their name is derived from the rubbery feel of their skin. The rubber boa is sometimes called the "two-headed snake" because on one end of its body is the small head with small, inconspicuous eyes and no distinct neck, while on the other end is the blunt tail, which resembles the head in shape, size, and color. The "spurs," or vestigial limbs, are larger on males and are more difficult to see on females. The scales of the rubber boa are small and smooth. The scales on their chin/throat area are smaller than the chin scales of other snake species in this region. Like rattlesnakes, rubber boas have vertically elliptical pupils, similar to the pupils of a house cat.

The color of rubber boas is generally uniform on the back and sides, ranging from very dark brown to olive green or pale tan. All color phases generally are cream-colored or yellow underneath.

Rubber boas can be identified by their behavior as well as by their anatomy. In Yellowstone and the Tetons, this species often is observed on cloudy days, lying in or along a trail paralleling a stream. When found, rubber boas frequently will not try to escape as most other snakes would. This species of snake is very docile and does not bite. They usually, but not always, move slowly. We have observed individuals that, when caught in the field, can be wrapped around a person's wrist where they may stay for hours.

JUVENILES.   The young are born live and average 22 cm (10 in.) in length. Juvenile rubber boas have often been described as looking like earthworms because of their tubular shape, inconspicuous eyes, and light brown to nearly pink coloration. Looking at a litter of recently hatched rubber boas in the hand is like looking at a handful of nightcrawlers, but upon closer inspection, these "worms" have eyes and very small scales. Despite their shiny appearance, they are not slimy like earthworms, but, like all snakes, are dry.

SIMILAR SPECIES.   Because of the eastern yellow-bellied racer's uniform grayish color, it is the only species with which a rubber boa might be confused in this region. However, racers are thinner, longer, have prominent eyes with round pupils, a pointed tail, large scales on their chins, are diurnal, and much faster moving (and hence are much harder to catch) than rubber boas.

Distribution
Rubber boas are found from southern British Columbia to the mountains of southern California, and east to western Montana and Wyoming (Stebbins 1985). They are known to occur in scattered locations in the mountains as far south as the San Bernardino Mountains of southern California (Erwin 1974). So little is known about this species of snake that it is still quite probable that many undocumented populations occur between the areas where it is now known to exist.

This species probably occurs throughout most of both Yellowstone and Grand Teton National Parks, with the possible exception of the highest portions of the mountain canyons of the Teton range. However, they have been reported from as high as 2620 m (8600 ft) elevation in Yellowstone, and they do occur in many (probably all) of the lower portions of the canyons on the east side of the Teton Range. Observations of rubber boas have been reported from the low-

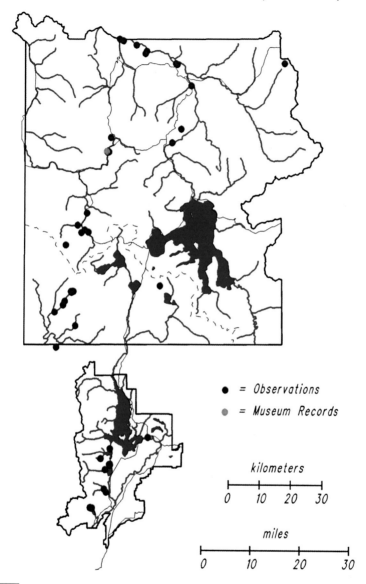

● = *Observations*

● = *Museum Records*

kilometers

0   10   20   30

miles

0   10   20   30

Rubber boas occur in a variety of locations from the warm, arid northern range of Yellowstone to the cool mountain wetlands of the Tetons to the south. So widely varying are the habitats in which this species occurs, and so infrequently is it encountered in the field, that we cannot adequately characterize a likely potential habitat to find this species in the region. Many places in both parks remain unsampled.

est elevation for the two national parks, near Gardiner, Montana, along the Yellowstone River at 1645 m (5400 ft) elevation.

Not until 1994 did a museum collection record exist for this species from either national park, and this animal was collected only because, when visiting Yellowstone Park, Stephen Sullivan (Carroll College, Helena, Montana) was aware of the importance of collecting a rubber boa and did so when he found one dead on the road. We have not yet encountered a rubber boa in either national park, so count yourselves among the more fortunate if you do. Because of the secretive habits of this snake, we do not have many widespread observation records in this region. Also interesting is the fact that, unlike virtually all other species included in this book, a significant proportion of recorded observations of rubber boas in Yellowstone and the Tetons are from backcountry areas, or areas away from roads. Specifically, the two major rubber boa "hot spots" are (1) on hiking trails near Three Rivers Junction in the Bechler region of southwestern Yellowstone National Park (25 km [14 mi] from the nearest road), and (2) Death Canyon near Phelps Lake in Grand Teton National Park (3 km [2 mi] from the nearest road). We speculate that these areas produce many boa sightings because the trails in these areas happen to pass through an area between a den, or hibernation site, and a water source and/or hunting area, possibly along a stream. This coincidence may be rare due to the small home range size rubber boas generally have.

Abundance/Status

Relatively few observations of rubber boas have been reported in Yellowstone and the Tetons. We suspect that the apparent rarity of this species may be due more to the nocturnal, fossorial (that is, burrowing) habits of rubber boas than to only a small number of individuals occurring here. A recent intensive study of a population of rubber boas in a small canyon in southeastern Idaho revealed that the size of the population probably approaches 150 individuals, even though only a few were ever seen at one time (Michael Dorcas, Idaho State University, personal communication, 1993).

Natural History

Most of what we know about the natural history of rubber boas in the northern intermountain west is due to the efforts of Michael Dorcas, a Ph.D. student at Idaho State University. He has used miniature, surgically implanted radio transmitters to study the ecology of this species near Pocatello, Idaho, on the southwestern edge of the Greater Yellowstone Ecosystem. Very little scientific literature is available on this species.

HABITAT.   We have found rubber boas from other areas in a wide variety of habitats, and they have been reported from a wide variety of habitats in the region covered by this book. Rubber boa habitat is generally characterized by having rocky areas for retreating underground, loose soil and/or leaf litter to burrow under, and, commonly, there are shrubs or trees nearby. These sites occur near riparian areas adjacent to streams and in meadows. Presumably these areas provide foraging habitat for a variety of prey, including small mammals (one of the boa's principal prey items).

Rubber boas are primarily fossorial, or closely associated with the ground, being found under leaf litter and in rodent burrows. This snake commonly burrows into loose soil with its head, and as a result, it does not have an opening at the front of the mouth for the tongue to protrude when tongue flicking or "tasting" its environment with its tongue (Hildebrand 1974). Therefore, it must actually elevate its snout slightly for tongue flicking to occur. This adaptation presumably keeps dirt out of the mouth of the boa. We have usually found boas in habitats near water. They are known to climb trees well and even raid bird nests and eat young or possibly eggs found there (Cooper et al. 1978).

Rubber boas can have small home range sizes compared to similar-sized snake species. Michael Dorcas (personal communication, 1993) found that many individuals never ventured farther than 100 m (100 yd) from their den site. One individual in Dorcas's study traveled over 500 m (500 yd) from the den site before he lost track of it. Also, individual snakes may not all use the same site for hibernation but may instead use nearby rodent burrows or rock crevices for hibernation.

ACTIVITY PATTERNS.   Near Pocatello, Idaho, rubber boas are generally active from April through October, although Dorcas has seen
some rubber boas active as late as November in warmer years. The
activity season of rubber boas in the parks is presumably shorter,
due to the cooler conditions at higher elevations.

Rubber boas are considered a nocturnal species, active primarily at night. Coupled with this is the fact that rubber boas spend
much of their time underground, in rodent burrows, or under leaf
litter on the forest floor. Also, individuals of this species are more
often found simply lying still or moving very slowly and are not
noticed moving about quickly, as many other kinds of snakes do.
Consequently, this snake is not often found without significant
effort, even in areas where it may actually be common (Hoyer
1974, Baxter and Stone 1985).

Rubber boas are remarkably cold tolerant. Like most other species of reptiles, rubber boas may be active at relatively warm temperatures. But unlike other reptiles, they may also be active at
very cool temperatures, as low as 6°C (40°F) (Michael Dorcas, personal communication, 1993). As mentioned previously, rubber
boas are most commonly observed moving very slowly or not at
all, and this may be especially true at such low temperatures.

Rubber boas can live for long periods of time. We have a live
female rubber boa that was captured as a large adult in 1977, over
17 years ago. The maximum life span of these animals has not
been well documented.

FEEDING HABITS.   Rubber boas are known to feed on a wide variety of prey, such as invertebrates, snakes, lizards, birds, mice,
voles, and shrews. One large individual of 71 cm (28 in.) in length
was captured in Midway Geyser Basin near Old Faithful and subsequently regurgitated a recently eaten mouse (Agerter 1932). Like
their larger relatives, the boas and pythons from the tropics, these
snakes are true constrictors of prey. Small rodents seem to be their
most frequent victims. Michael Dorcas (personal communication,
1993) observed remains of a shrew in a juvenile rubber boa, which
is remarkable considering the apparent fragility of a young rubber
boa and the fact that, although tiny in size, shrews are known to
be very aggressive animals. In laboratory studies, adult rubber

boas have been reported to feed on juvenile mice in their nest, while using their tail to fend off the mother (Nussbaum et al. 1983). Despite their reputation for moving slowly, rubber boas are able to move quickly when pursuing prey (Borell 1931).

ENEMIES/DEFENSE.   Rubber boas attempt to defend themselves from attack by using their headlike tail as a diversion. The snake forms a coil with its head at the bottom while waving the tail in the air and even "striking" with it in defense, as other snake species strike with their head. The tip of the tail of the boa is formed of several fused, conical vertebrae, which stand up well to such abuses. Frequently, wild rubber boas exhibit significant scarring on the tips of their tails. These snakes can also emit a strong musk scent from their vent when agitated, which may serve to deter potential predators, such as badgers, raccoons, martens, hawks, and owls. We have even received a report in western Idaho of a large boreal toad attempting (eventually unsuccessfully) to eat a small rubber boa (Al Larson, Boise, Idaho, personal communication, 1993).

REPRODUCTION/DEVELOPMENT.   In the Willamette Valley of western Oregon, courtship usually occurs from late April to early May (Nussbaum et al. 1983). In Yellowstone and the Tetons, courtship presumably occurs later in the year because of cooler conditions. Females give birth to small numbers of young, usually from two to eight individuals. The young are normally born in September in other parts of their range (Nussbaum et al. 1983). Pregnant rubber boas gather in a rocky area for most of the summer months while gestation occurs. Because development of the embryos is generally dependent on body temperature of the mother, gestating females generally attempt to maintain a constant elevated body temperature near 27°C (80°F) by moving in and out of the sun and moving underground at night. In 1993 (an unusually cold year) two rubber boas at the Pocatello site failed to complete their pregnancy, and the young were not born alive the following year. Females apparently do not reproduce every year (Michael Dorcas, personal communication, 1993).

Bull Snake
Pituophis catenifer sayi

Bull snakes are large, powerful snakes that constrict their prey, mostly small mammals. These snakes have a tan or yellow base color with brown to black blotches down the length of the body on the back and sides. Differentiating bull snakes from other snake species of the region is relatively simple. Even the somewhat similar prairie rattlesnake is different, with a larger head and narrower neck, and rattles on the end of the tail. Bull snakes are common along the lower Yellowstone and Gardner Rivers near Mammoth, Wyoming, in the northern portion of Yellowstone Park.

The bull snake is the subspecies of the gopher snake *(Pituophis catenifer)* that is known to occur in Yellowstone National Park. This subspecies occurs primarily east of the continental divide. The subspecies of the gopher snake west of the continental divide in the northern intermountain west is called the Great Basin gopher snake *(Pituophis catenifer deserticola)*. This is the subspecies that occurs in the southern portion of the Greater Yellowstone Ecosystem and potentially could occur in Grand Teton National Park. These two subspecies are similar in appearance, with relatively minor differences in scalation and color pattern (see below). Bull snakes are members of the family Colubridae, the largest family of snakes.

Description

ADULTS. The bull snake is the longest snake found in the region, with lengths of adults occasionally exceeding 2 m (6 ft) in Wyoming (Baxter and Stone 1985). This snake has a tan or yellow base color with brown blotches in a pattern down the back. (It is generally darker than the Great Basin gopher snake to the south and west.) The brown blotched pattern is sometimes bordered with black. Toward the posterior end of the animal, the blotches eventually become rings around the tail and are nearly black. On each side of the snake are smaller, longer spots which alternate in their position along the body with the blotches on the back. The belly is white or yellow, with occasional spotting. The color pattern on the head is variable, but usually a black stripe, or mask, extends from the corner of the jaw up through the eye (Baxter and Stone 1985). Bull snakes have keeled (ridged) scales, which give these snakes a "textured" appearance. They have a protruding scale at the tip of the snout (the rostral scale), which is narrower than in the Great Basin gopher snake.

JUVENILES. Juvenile bull snakes are similar in appearance to adults.

SIMILAR SPECIES.   Bull snakes are relatively easy to distinguish from the other species of snakes in the parks. Rubber boas lack any pattern; both species of garter snakes have stripes; and rattlesnakes have rattles, large heads with narrow necks, facial pits, and vertical pupils. However, bull snakes have a pattern that is similar to the pattern of prairie rattlesnakes, and their defensive behavior resembles that of rattlesnakes in several ways (see section on *enemies and defense* below).

Distribution
The bull snake is widely distributed throughout western North America, from southern Canada to northern Mexico, and west to the Pacific Coast from Wisconsin and the Great Plains states (Stebbins 1985). It may occur commonly within its distribution in the region, which includes the lowest elevations of Yellowstone National Park along the Yellowstone and Gardner Rivers near where they leave the park. It is generally restricted to areas below 2040 m (6700 ft) elevation, which includes the Hoodoos, just uphill of Mammoth Hot Springs on the Mammoth-to-Norris road. We have heard third-hand reports of this species near and upstream of Sheepeater Cliffs, a short distance farther up the Gardner River drainage from the Hoodoos. It would not surprise us to find that it occurs there as well. We have commonly observed bull snakes along the Gardner River near the Boiling River on the Mammoth-to-Gardiner road. They also can be found in the Mammoth campground, and one individual was reported living under Liberty Cap, a geothermal formation in the Mammoth Hot Springs area. Every year, bull snakes are observed in and around the Administrative Headquarters of Yellowstone in Mammoth, and some individuals are found dead on the road near the YACC camp just up the road (south) from the Mammoth area. Turner (1955) also reported this snake species at Reese Creek, downstream from the town of Gardiner, Montana.

It is not entirely clear how far upstream on the Yellowstone River bull snakes occur. We have only one report of a bull snake up the Yellowstone River as far as the Blacktail Patrol Cabin. We have many reports of rattlesnakes in the Crevice Creek area, which is downstream of Blacktail Patrol Cabin. The presence of

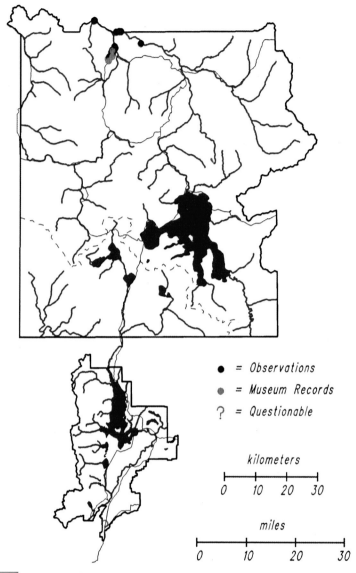

● = Observations
● = Museum Records
? = Questionable

kilometers

0   10   20   30

miles

0   10   20   30

Bull snakes occur in the northern portion of Yellowstone Park, from
Gardiner, Montana along the Yellowstone River upstream to Crevice
Creek, and upstream along the Gardner River to above Mammoth Hot
Springs. This species has also been reported in the southern portion of the
Tetons. Many places remain unsampled.

rattlesnakes at Crevice Creek suggests to us that bull snakes could be found there as well. Rattlesnakes tend to draw more attention and are more likely to be reported than bull snakes, even though both species are often found together. Bull snakes apparently occur at higher elevations than rattlesnakes in the Gardner River drainage and therefore may occur even farther up the Yellowstone River drainage than rattlesnakes. However, this is contrary to observations made by George Baxter (University of Wyoming, personal communication, 1993) in other parts of Wyoming, where the prairie rattlesnake occurs at higher elevations than the bull snake. We need better information on the maximal points where bull snakes occur upstream along the Yellowstone and Gardner Rivers.

We have received one report of this species for Grand Teton National Park: a dead individual on the road near Gros Ventre Junction, near the southern end of Blacktail Butte. Because this site is west of the continental divide, the reported individual probably would have been a Great Basin gopher snake (*Pituophis catenifer deserticola*). We cannot comment on the validity of this single observation of this species in the Tetons, or whether it occurred there naturally or was transported from elsewhere and released or deposited there. However, given how little is known about amphibians and reptiles in the region covered by this book and the fact that gopher snakes occur nearby (only 22 km [14 mi] downstream on the Snake River near Hoback Junction), it seems possible to us that the gopher snake may also occur in Grand Teton National Park but simply has never been confirmed. Indeed, the southern end of Blacktail Butte would be a likely habitat type in which to find this snake. Carpenter (1953a) reported that this species likely occurred in the Hoback Junction area, but offered no comment on the likelihood of their occurrence farther north.

Abundance/Status

Baxter and Stone (1985) reported that the bull snake is declining in numbers in Wyoming because of human development, mainly roads, where snakes get run over by automobiles. Also, Turner (1955) stated that this species was less common than in earlier times, being rarely seen in Yellowstone. These reported declines may be a result of the probability that snakes were and still are

Here along the Gardner River near the Boiling River between Mammoth, Wyoming, and Gardiner, Montana, we found several bull snakes foraging in the riparian habitat immediately adjacent to the stream channel. These snakes live only at the lowest elevations in Yellowstone, in and around sagebrush habitats, where temperatures are warm enough to make a living.

feared, usually for no good reason, and are subsequently killed. In August 1954, the Mammoth campground caretaker brought a bull snake into captivity for the remainder of that summer season for fear that the animal, which had a habit of sunning itself in conspicuous places, would be killed by an ignorant visitor (Turner 1955). Today, however, most people visiting national parks are advised to leave everything as they see it for the next visitor to enjoy. Despite the fact that some bull snakes are still accidentally run over on roads in Yellowstone, it is our experience that they may be locally common.

Natural History
HABITAT.   Bull snakes are found in dry grassland and sagebrush habitats typical of the lower Yellowstone River valley near Gardiner, Montana. We have found them frequently in green grassy areas along the lower Gardner River. Bull snakes can, to some extent, dig with the snout, and they are good climbers (Linder and

Fichter 1977). We have not identified winter denning sites for this species in Yellowstone National Park, but we received a report of a hibernaculum for bull snakes and rattlesnakes upstream on Bear Creek just north of the park boundary. Elsewhere in its range, the bull snake has been confirmed to hibernate with other snake species, including rattlesnakes and garter snakes. However, we have not personally observed bull snakes at the prairie rattlesnake den with which we are most familiar in Yellowstone National Park, near Stephens Creek.

ACTIVITY PATTERNS.   Elsewhere in its range, males of this species usually emerge from hibernation first, and females follow, all over a period of four to six weeks (Nussbaum et al. 1983). In Utah, individuals of this species hibernate from 180 to 250 days out of the year (Parker and Brown 1980). In the northern, low-elevation areas of Yellowstone, emergence of bull snakes probably begins as early as late April or May, possibly slightly sooner than rattlesnakes. We have observed them hundreds of meters (yards) from what we perceived to be potential den sites on Deckard Flats on the north side of the Yellowstone River in mid-May. At the same time on Deckard Flats, rattlesnakes were still aggregated near the mouths of the potential den sites. We also have seen bull snakes active and apparently foraging along the banks of the Gardner River near Boiling River in May, while rattlesnakes were still associated with the Stephens Creek den site 7 km (4 mi) distant. Retreat to the den site in the fall probably occurs in September or October.

Because of the cool nighttime temperatures in the northern portions of Yellowstone National Park, the activity of these snakes is probably restricted to the day or early evening. In southern Idaho, we have observed gopher snakes active at 2:00 A.M. during hot weather.

FEEDING HABITS.   The main prey items of bull snakes are small mammals such as ground squirrels, wood rats, mice, and small rabbits. They also will eat birds and lizards on occasion (Nussbaum et al. 1983). Turner (1955) reported that bull snakes in Yellowstone likely eat chipmunks, pocket gophers, voles, and ground squirrels. Elmore (1954 *cited in* Turner 1955) described a bull snake eating a ground squirrel in Yellowstone.

Bull snakes are powerful constrictors, wrapping coils around their prey or pressing prey against the walls of burrows or against rocks. The prey are killed by suffocation when their lungs cannot expand because of the pressure around them. They are not killed by being crushed to death.

ENEMIES/DEFENSE.   Bull snakes may be eaten by a number of predators, including badgers and coyotes. However, birds of prey, such as hawks and eagles, usually pose the greatest threat to this and many other species of snakes. In the canyons of the Snake River in south-central Idaho, gopher snakes (the western relative of the bull snake) made up over 60% of the mass of prey delivered to nestlings by red-tail hawk adults (Grothe 1992).

Bull snakes have several effective defensive mechanisms, including defensive behavior similar to the more dangerous rattlesnake. When threatened, bull snakes will often coil and flatten their heads into a more triangular shape. They also may shake the tip of the tail, similar to a rattlesnake. They often will hiss loudly before or during strikes (which are mostly bluffs). A ridge of cartilage in the trachea (windpipe) oscillates back and forth, acting as a mechanical amplifier. Presumably, the bull snake gets its name from this hissing noise, which to some people sounds like an angry bull. To some observers, it also sounds like the rattle of a rattlesnake. Bull snakes may even bite, but they are not venomous and have rather small teeth designed more for simply holding small prey items than for cutting. They usually will calm down after being handled for a short time. Like the garter snakes, little chance exists of a bull snake doing any kind of harm to a person, but its display can be frightening. Because of its behavior and appearance, this species is often mistaken for a rattlesnake by persons unfamiliar with snakes.

REPRODUCTION/DEVELOPMENT.   Mating probably occurs shortly after emergence from hibernation. Elsewhere in their range, females lay from 4 to 20 eggs in rocky crevices or rodent burrows in south-facing slopes in late June or early July (Nussbaum et al.

1983). Females shed their outer layer of skin about six days before egg laying. They may use the same nest site in successive years, and several females may use a common nest site. Incubation time of eggs is dependent on temperature and may take up to two months. The egg itself is usually white or cream-colored and oblong, measuring 3 cm by 6 cm (1.2 in. by 2.4 in.) (Nussbaum et al. 1983, Baxter and Stone 1985). Hatchlings shed for the first time about 16 days after hatching and grow rapidly for the first two to three years of life before slowing down (Nussbaum et al. 1983). Males mature at two to three years of age, and females at three to five years of age.

Stories of bull snakes mating and hybridizing with rattlesnakes are untrue. However, bull snakes and rattlesnakes can share the same hibernaculum, and stories of bull snakes killing rattlesnakes can be true, as Vince Cobb (Idaho State University, personal communication, 1993) has observed in southeast Idaho. This reputation, coupled with the fact that bull snakes eat rodents considered "undesirable" in farming areas, has fortunately allowed this snake species to sometimes receive preferential treatment from people who perceive them as "good." In Yellowstone and the Tetons, visitors are encouraged to shed their notion of "good" and "bad" animals, and simply try to see all organisms for what they are: interesting creatures that are making a living as they have since long before humans arrived.

Wandering Garter Snake
Thamnophis elegans vagrans

Wandering garter snakes are probably the most commonly encountered snake species in the region, because they are widespread throughout both parks, common where they occur, and active during the midday hours. This species has yellow stripes along the body typical of most garter snake species, with a darker checkered pattern over a green, brown, or gray base color. The valley garter snake also has yellow stripes, but with a solid dark green or black base color with red marks on the sides, and is restricted in its distribution in the region. Wandering garter snakes are usually found close to surface water and eat a variety of prey, from insects to fish.

123

The wandering garter snake is the subspecies of the western terrestrial garter snake (*Thamnophis elegans*) that occurs in the Greater Yellowstone Ecosystem. It is sometimes incorrectly called a water snake because it is often found in or near water. It is a member of the large family of "harmless" snakes called Colubridae.

Description

ADULTS. Wandering garter snakes are medium-sized snakes, ranging up to about 75 cm (30 in.) in length (Baxter and Stone 1985). Females can be longer and heavier than males. Newborn garter snakes range from 15 to 20 cm (6 to 8 in.) in length (Turner 1955, Nussbaum et al. 1983).

Wandering garter snakes vary in color. They have an olive green, brown, or gray base color with three yellow stripes running the length of the body; one down the middle of the back, and one each down the sides. The stripes are not always bold or conspicuous and may not be immediately visible. Alternating rows of dark squares or spots occur between the stripes on the backs and sides. The underside of this snake is usually unmarked or lightly speckled and light gray. The wandering garter snake usually has eight upper labial (lip) scales. However, we have occasionally observed wandering garter snakes with only seven upper labial scales on one or the other side of the head. The dorsal scales are keeled (ridged).

JUVENILES. Young wandering garter snakes generally look like miniature versions of the adults, although their colors are usually brighter and their patterns are more distinct.

SIMILAR SPECIES. The wandering garter snake can be differentiated from the valley garter snake (*Thamnophis sirtalis fitchi*), also found in the area, by three main characteristics: the wandering garter snake's lighter, more variable base color and checkered pattern; less distinct, yellow longitudinal stripes; and, most importantly, the *lack* of bright red flecking on each side of the snake along the anterior two-thirds of the body. The valley garter snake usually has only seven upper labial scales. The valley garter snake is restricted in distribution and abundance in the parks. Our experience shows that if you see a garter snake in Grand Teton National Park, it will usually be a wandering garter snake; in Yellowstone, it will almost always be a wandering garter snake.

Distribution

The wandering garter snake occurs throughout most of the western United States and southwestern Canada. It is the most widely distributed reptile in Yellowstone and Grand Teton National Parks. It is known to occur from the lowest elevation in the area, near Gardiner, Montana, at 1615 m (5300 ft) elevation, up to 2450 m (8038 ft) elevation and probably occurs even higher. This is one of the few species for which we have a record in the upper portions of the canyons on the east side of the Teton range in Grand Teton National Park.

Abundance/Status

Wandering garter snakes are the most abundant and commonly observed reptile in the parks. Because they communally hibernate, they may be seen in considerable numbers (dozens or hundreds) at their denning sites, especially in the spring. We also have observed many garter snakes in the summer when they converge at ponds to feed on transforming amphibians.

Natural History

HABITAT.   The habitat of wandering garter snakes varies seasonally. From late fall through early spring they communally hibernate, usually in rocky areas with a southern exposure and near water. In other parts of their range, we have observed wandering garter snakes hibernating with other snake species, including rubber boas, bull snakes, racers, common garter snakes, and/or rattlesnakes. These snakes usually breed in the spring, near the den site, and then later disperse to foraging sites located near water. They

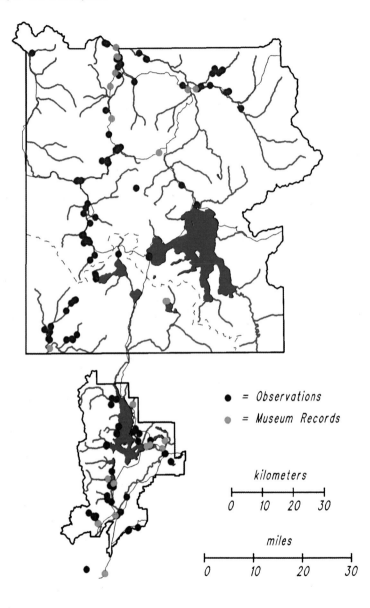

= *Observations*

= *Museum Records*

kilometers

0   10   20   30

miles

0   10   20   30

Wandering garter snakes occur in a variety of locations from the warm, arid northern range of Yellowstone to the cool mountain wetlands of the Tetons to the south. This species is usually found near surface water of some kind. Many places in both parks remain unsampled.

Wet meadows with adjacent streams or ponds for foraging and rocky outcroppings nearby for shelter are typical areas where wandering garter snakes can make a living. We have found several individuals of this snake species here at an old oxbow off the Snake River near Yellowstone's South Entrance, an amphibian monitoring site. We have also found tiger salamanders, boreal toads, spotted frogs, and chorus frogs at this site.

also will hibernate in areas disturbed by humans (for example, at the base of bridge supports, road banks, and under building foundations). They probably shuttle between daytime foraging areas and nearby, nighttime retreat sites in burrows or under rocks or logs.

Wandering garter snakes are both terrestrial and aquatic. Turner (1955) stated: "Though these garter snakes are abundant in Yellowstone, it should not be concluded that they are found in widely differing habitats. As a matter of fact these snakes are encountered almost invariably along streams or rivers or near ponds." The same can be said about the Tetons. Carpenter (1953a) reported that in the Jackson Hole valley the wandering garter snake "was found less frequently along the streams and floodplains than was [the common garter snake]; however, both species were found together near pools and marshes." We have observed that these snakes may be associated with geothermally influenced areas (for example, Storm Point on the north shore of Yellowstone Lake). The effect of thermal areas on the distribution, activity patterns, and life history characteristics of garter snakes in Yellowstone National Park promises to be a fascinating research topic.

ACTIVITY PATTERNS.   Wandering garter snakes in this region may be active from April through October. One individual of this species was seen in the Upper Geyser Basin near Old Faithful on April 16 and had been out for some time, the observer concluded, because it already had shed its skin once (Yeager 1926). Another observer saw a total of 16 garter snakes somewhere in the vicinity of Old Faithful during May in a small clearing near some rocks surrounded by snow (Jacobson 1926). We have even heard a report of an active garter snake during February in the Mammoth Hot Springs area.

Wandering garter snakes are generally active during the day. Elsewhere in their range, they usually do not emerge from retreat sites until they can obtain body temperatures of at least 15°C (59°F). If possible, they usually will behaviorally regulate their body temperatures between 25 and 35°C (77 and 95°F) (Peterson 1987). However, we have seen individuals active after dark in and adjacent to the Firehole River, perhaps not coincidentally near warm water runoff from hot springs, possibly obtaining body heat from the runoff.

FEEDING HABITS.   Wandering garter snakes feed on a wide variety of prey. By gently forcing individual snakes to regurgitate their stomach contents, we have found snails, slugs, leeches, tiger salamanders, western toads, chorus frogs, spotted frogs, and voles in these snakes in Yellowstone and the Tetons. We saw one individual eating a sculpin (a small fish) along the Bechler River in Yellowstone. Others have reported this snake species eating trout (Reinhard 1930, and Breitenbach 1951 *cited in* Turner 1955), salamanders (Turner 1952 *cited in* Turner 1955), and young birds (Lystrup 1952 *cited in* Turner 1955) in Yellowstone. Wandering garter snakes may even climb trees to prey upon birds (Dr. Richard Hutto, University of Montana, personal communication, 1992). Carpenter (1953a) reported that toads, chorus frogs, and sculpin were included in the diet of wandering garter snakes in Jackson Hole. These snakes can gorge themselves on transforming toads or frogs if they find such aggregations and will also eat tadpoles. They can rapidly pursue prey; one individual was observed near Ice Lake Reservoir chasing a vole for 5 m (15 ft) before catching it (Steve Hill, Montana State University, personal communication, 1994). We have even documented this species eating carrion (for example, a dead salamander) in other parts of its range.

Although garter snakes have well-developed eyes, they probably rely most heavily on their senses of smell and taste (chemoreception) to locate prey. Indeed, experimental studies indicate that common garter snakes can successfully capture prey and return to nighttime retreats even with their eyes covered (Dr. James Gillingham, Central Michigan University, personal communication, 1985).

Usually, garter snakes simply swallow their prey alive. However, they may coil around large, struggling prey items and bite them repeatedly. Their saliva apparently is toxic to some prey items but does not pose a threat to humans.

ENEMIES/DEFENSE. A variety of animals may prey on garter snakes, including large fish, snakes (rubber boas and other wandering garter snakes), birds (for example, herons, hawks, ravens, and magpies), carnivorous mammals (for example, badgers and raccoons), and even predaceous beetles (on small snakes). A bear was observed killing a garter snake near Fishing Bridge on August 5, 1953 (Turner 1955) but did not attempt to eat it. These snakes will emit a musky fluid along with their feces when threatened or handled, presumably to ward off potential predators. They also may bite when handled, although their teeth cannot do much harm to a human.

The wandering garter snake can move swiftly when attempting to escape. It has been our experience that the snake's yellow stripes can deceive the eye into thinking the snake is not moving or is moving more slowly than it is. This deception is especially true when the head of the snake is not visible in tall grass and can cause the person trying to capture it to grab far to the rear of the snake or to miss it altogether. This color pattern may be an adaptation to avoid capture by potential predators and may cause predators to miss when trying to grab the garter snake (Brodie 1990). The common garter snake also seems to possess this ability to deceive potential predators.

REPRODUCTION/DEVELOPMENT.   We have received reports indicating that in Yellowstone breeding usually occurs in the spring soon after the snakes emerge from hibernation. A female presumably attracts males by releasing a chemical attractant called a pheromone. Several males may simultaneously attempt to mate with a single female, forming "mating balls." Pregnant garter snakes are less active than nonpregnant snakes and generally spend most of their time attempting to stay warm (about 30°C) during the course of pregnancy (Peterson 1987, Charland 1991, Peterson et al. 1993). Females of this species bear 4 to 19 live young (Nussbaum et al. 1983) in August or early September (Turner 1955). Because of the relatively short activity season in the parks, female garter snakes probably cannot capture enough prey to gain enough energy to reproduce every year.

Valley Garter Snake

Thamnophis sirtalis fitchi

The valley garter snake is restricted in distribution to Grand Teton National Park and the southwest portion of Yellowstone. It is distinguishable
from its close relative, the wandering garter snake, by its brighter yellow
stripes down the body, solid, dark green or black base color, and red checkered marks along its side. Valley garter snakes are even more closely associated with surface water than wandering garter snakes, and are sometimes
thought of as specializing in preying on amphibians. We believe this snake
species has declined in abundance over the last 40 years in the region.

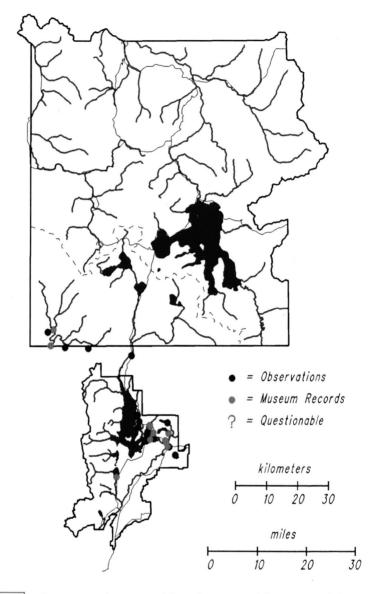

● = *Observations*

● = *Museum Records*

? = *Questionable*

kilometers

0   10   20   30

miles

0   10   20   30

Valley garter snakes occurred throughout most of the Tetons and the southwest corner of Yellowstone. This species appears to have declined markedly in the Tetons over the last 40 years. This species may also occur to the north in Yellowstone Park, but it has yet to be confirmed. Many places in both parks remain unsampled.

The valley garter snake is the subspecies of the common garter snake (*Thamnophis sirtalis*) that is known to occur in Grand Teton and Yellowstone National Parks. It is more closely related to the wandering garter snake (*Thamnophis elegans vagrans*) than to other species of snakes in the parks. The garter snakes are members of the family Colubridae.

Description

ADULTS.   Valley garter snakes are medium-sized snakes, reaching total lengths of up to 86 cm (34 in.) in the Greater Yellowstone Ecosystem (Carpenter 1953a). They have a nearly black background color. Set off against the dark background are three bright yellow, longitudinal stripes running the length of the body; one stripe runs down the middle of the back, and one stripe runs down each side. Perhaps the most important distinguishing characteristic of this subspecies in our region are the irregular red spots along the sides. The underside can be pale yellow or bluish gray, tending toward a cream color anteriorly. Valley garter snakes usually have seven upper labial (lip) scales. Their dorsal scales are keeled (ridged).

JUVENILES.   Juvenile valley garter snakes generally look like smaller versions of the adults.

SIMILAR SPECIES.   Although the valley garter snake is most likely to be confused with the wandering garter snake, it is not difficult to separate them. As mentioned previously, the wandering garter snake has a duskier base color with a checkered pattern, less bold, sometimes obscured yellow stripes, and *no* red spots along its sides. Also, wandering garter snakes usually have eight upper labial scales on each side of their face.

Distribution

The common garter snake is the most widely distributed reptile in North America. It is found in most of the lower 48 states, but is absent in much of the desert southwest. It has the northernmost distribution of any reptile in North America, extending into the Northwest Territories, Canada. The subspecies of common garter snake found in Yellowstone and the Tetons (that is, the valley garter snake) is found throughout most of the northwestern United States west of the continental divide (Stebbins 1985).

In Grand Teton National Park, valley garter snakes have been found throughout the Jackson Hole valley, including Pilgrim Creek, Two Ocean Lakes and Buffalo River, and the Snake River both downstream and upstream of Jackson Lake Dam. We have no reports of the valley garter snake further south in the Tetons near Moose or Jackson, although we suspect they may occur there because they are known to occur both upstream and downstream of this area. In the region covered by this book, the valley garter is known to occur up to 2100 m (6897 ft), about 300 m (900 ft) lower in elevation than the wandering garter snake reaches. Like most other species included in this book, valley garter snakes have not been reported from the high-elevation canyons on the east side of the Teton Range in Grand Teton National Park. We think this area may be too high in elevation for valley garter snakes to reproduce, even though they are found at the canyon mouths in Jackson Hole itself. However, we will not know how far up the canyons they extend until surveys are conducted.

In Yellowstone, we have observed valley garter snakes only in the Falls River drainage in the Bechler region, which is in the southwest corner of the park. They also have been observed just three miles south of the South Entrance to Yellowstone Park along the Snake River (Carpenter 1953a) but have not yet been recorded north of the park border in the Snake River drainage. They apparently are also found around Grassy Lake Reservoir, which lies in the Falls River drainage, between Grand Teton and Yellowstone National Parks.

Two reports exist for this species east of the continental divide in our region. A garter snake with red markings was seen along the lower section of the Gardner River at the north end of Yellowstone National Park (Yeager 1929). And in May 1992, Susan Seibert (West Yellowstone, Montana, personal communication, 1992) observed a garter snake with red markings along the bike trail into

Lone Star Geyser near Old Faithful. If common garter snakes occur naturally at these localities, they probably belong to the subspecies that occurs primarily east of the continental divide, the red-sided garter snake (*Thamnophis sirtalis parietalis*).

Abundance/Status

On the basis of Carpenter's field notes and the number of museum specimens, valley garter snakes appear to have been common in the past. However, despite considerable time spent in the field during the past several years, we have not yet observed this species in Grand Teton National Park and know of only a few recent observations by others. George Baxter (University of Wyoming, personal communication, 1993) has also noted a decline in valley garter snakes in Jackson Hole over the course of his career. We do not know why this apparent decline has occurred, but it may be significant that leopard frogs and toads also have declined or disappeared from Jackson Hole. These three species also appear to have declined in southeastern Idaho (Charles R. Peterson, unpublished data).

Natural History

HABITAT.   In the parks, valley garter snakes are usually found closely associated with permanent surface water. They are most commonly found in the floodplains along the Snake River and other rivers in the valley floor of Grand Teton National Park (Carpenter 1953a). The single specimen of this species we collected in Yellowstone was on a trail near the banks of the Falls River. Wandering garter snakes may also occur in these same areas. In other parts of their range, we have observed valley garter snakes hibernating with other snake species, including wandering garter snakes, racers, and rubber boas. Hibernacula are similar to those of wandering garter snakes. Carpenter (1953a) saw four pregnant females on a river floodplain near a burrow under a log on July 12, 1951.

ACTIVITY PATTERNS.   Adults emerge in spring as soon as the weather warms sufficiently. Presumably, this could be as early as

Common garter snakes used to be commonly found 40 years ago along the Snake River in Grand Teton National Park. These snakes may have occurred at one time here along the river and floodplain wetlands near Lower Schwabacher Landing, a popular boat launch along the near bank of the Snake River in the middle of the valley in Grand Teton National Park. We have in recent times observed boreal toads and wandering garter snakes here, but we have not found common garter snakes anywhere in the Tetons in recent years. The wetland complex upstream of where the river swings east towards the parking area is an amphibian monitoring site.

Near Bechler Meadows in the southwest corner of Yellowstone Park is where we found the only valley garter snake we have encountered in our six years of searching in the region. Despite the frequency with which Chuck Carpenter found this snake species in Jackson Hole (now in Grand Teton National Park) 40 years ago, we have yet to observe it here.

April but more likely occurs in May. They may retreat to the den sites at similar times as wandering garter snakes. Valley garter snakes are generally active during the day.

FEEDING HABITS. Valley garter snakes have a more limited diet than do wandering garter snakes. Carpenter (1953a) found toads, chorus frogs, and fish remains were included in the diet of the valley garter snake in Jackson Hole. Elsewhere, this species frequently feeds on earthworms. Interestingly, this species is so well adapted to eating amphibians, it can eat relatively poisonous species of amphibians like the western toad (which has parotoid glands secreting toxins) and not suffer ill effects. In fact, valley garter snakes from within the range of the roughskin newt (*Taricha granulosa*) in the northwestern United States are 2,000 times less susceptible to the toxins in the skin of the newt than are mice (Nussbaum et al. 1983).

ENEMIES/DEFENSE. Valley garter snakes are probably preyed upon by a wide variety of predators, including fish, birds, and carnivorous mammals. They use a variety of behaviors to defend themselves. As with the wandering garter snake, the valley garter snake can move swiftly when attempting to escape, and their yellow stripes may aid them in avoiding capture by predators (see description of the wandering garter snake). Valley garter snakes may strike if cornered and may bite when handled, but their bite is not dangerous. They often will inflate their lung (they only have one), increasing the amount of red markings exposed. Like other garter snakes, they will release a potent musk from glands at the base of their tail, and the contents of their cloaca (feces and uric acid).

REPRODUCTION/DEVELOPMENT. These snakes generally mate in spring, soon after emergence from hibernation. Elsewhere in their range, fall mating is known to occur in addition to spring mating. Males emerge from hibernation first and await the females. Multiple males often court a single female. Following mating, a copulatory plug may form in the female's cloaca and prevent her from mating with other males, at least for several days (Devine 1975, 1977). Ovulation presumably occurs in May or early June. The young are born alive, late in the summer. We observed that a large female from southeastern Idaho gave birth to eight young. Elsewhere in their range, garter snakes have been known to give birth to over 80 young (Nussbaum et al. 1983).

Prairie Rattlesnake
Crotalis viridis viridis

Sometimes feared but rarely a threat to most park visitors, rattlesnakes can be common where they occur at the lowest elevations in Yellowstone Park along the Yellowstone River near Gardiner, Montana, and upstream. Rattlesnakes can be distinguished from other snake species by their dusky gray or brown color with darker blotches along the back, a broad head with a distinct neck, a thick body toward the rear of the animal, and the characteristic rattle on the end of the tail. We know of only two snake bites in the 120-year history of the park. Most bites occur after a purposeful interaction with a rattlesnake by a person. If you leave them alone (like most wildlife, they are protected in the park), they will leave you alone.

The prairie rattlesnake is the subspecies of the western rattlesnake (*Crotalus viridis*) that occurs in Yellowstone National Park. It is a member of the family Viperidae (the vipers) and the subfamily Crotalinae (the pit vipers). The rattlesnakes are distinguished by the rattle at the end of their tails. The prairie rattlesnake is the only dangerously venomous snake found in the region covered by this book.

Description

ADULTS.   The prairie rattlesnake is a relatively large, stout-bodied snake. Individuals may grow fairly long in Yellowstone; we have observed snakes exceeding 1.3 m (48 in.) in length. Like most members of the viper family, this snake has a triangular-shaped head (when viewed from the top) with a narrow neck region and a thick mid-body region with a short tail that tapers quickly, ending in the distinctive rattle. It has a vertically elliptical pupil, similar to the pupil of a house cat's eye.

The prairie rattlesnake in this region is tan, gray, or even greenish brown, with darker blotches in a pattern down the back. The blotches are sometimes outlined in white and may form complete rings around the tail. The underside of the prairie rattlesnake is white or light yellow and generally is without a pattern. A great deal of variation in coloration occurs, even within the same population. The scales are strongly keeled (ridged). The keeled scales give the snake a roughened or textured look.

JUVENILES.   Young rattlesnakes look much like the adults but usually are more brightly colored.

SIMILAR SPECIES.   The only other snake species that the rattlesnake might be confused with in this region is the bull snake. Bull snakes lack a rattle, lack facial pits, have a head that is less wide with a less distinct neck region, and have round pupils. The rattlesnake also tends to have less contrast between its base color and the pattern color, but this is not always the case, especially with juveniles.

Distribution

This species ranges throughout the western United States, from the eastern Great Plains westward to the Pacific Ocean, and from southern Canada south to northern Mexico. The western rattle-snake, *C. viridis*, is a complex of several subspecies. The prairie rattlesnake subspecies (*C. v. viridis*), which is found in Yellowstone National Park, occurs across the Great Plains from southern Canada to northern Mexico, and from eastern South Dakota, Nebraska, and central Kansas westward to the Rocky Mountains, including east-central Idaho (Stebbins 1985). It is found in warm, arid, lower elevation areas throughout its range, usually below 2300 m (7000 ft) elevation in Wyoming, but occasionally as high as 2750 m (8400 ft) (Baxter and Stone 1985).

In this region, the prairie rattlesnake is found only in the extreme northern part of Yellowstone National Park where the Yellowstone River leaves the park. The highest elevation at which it is known to occur is 1700 m (6000 ft), but we have reports of rattlesnakes just outside the park up to 2140 m (7000 ft). It could be found higher with the right habitat conditions. Rattlesnakes have not been reported in Grand Teton National Park. Because this species usually receives much attention where it is found, we think that rattlesnakes likely do not occur there.

Unlike bull snakes, prairie rattlesnakes are currently not likely to be found very far up the Gardner River drainage in Yellowstone National Park. We do not have confirmed reports from the Boiling River area or Mammoth Hot Springs, although bull snakes do occur in these places. We do have an unconfirmed report of a rattlesnake near Mammoth in 1993. It seems that rattlesnakes occur at higher elevations in the Yellowstone River drainage than in the Gardner River drainage, which could be due to a difference in habitat availability. For example, if more flat, open sagebrush habitat occurred up the Gardner River drainage, more rattlesnakes might also be present. It is also possible that rattlesnakes historically occurred at least somewhat farther upstream along the Gardner

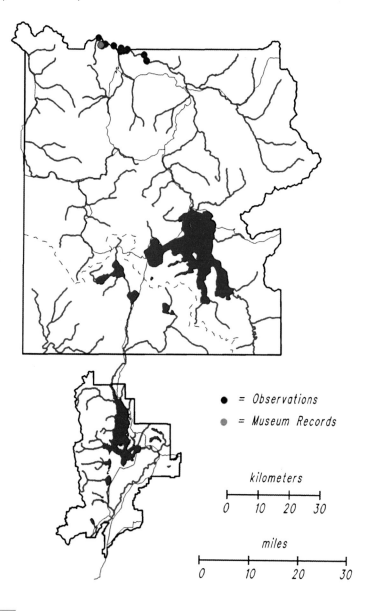

● = *Observations*

● = *Museum Records*

Prairie rattlesnakes occur in the northern portion of Yellowstone Park, from Gardiner, Montana along the Yellowstone River upstream to Crevice Creek. The upper altitudinal limit of this species here remains uncertain.

River, but that they are no longer found there. Evidence exists to support this hypothesis. Historian Aubrey Haines audiotaped interviews that are now archived in the Yellowstone Library (Lee Whittlesey, Yellowstone National Park Historical Archivist, personal communication, 1994). They include a discussion by former stagecoach drivers in the park about the relatively common occurrence of rattlesnakes along the Gardner River earlier this century.

We know of at least five areas where reports of rattlesnakes are concentrated. These areas may each be associated with a common den site for that area and are associated with drainages along the Yellowstone River: Stephens Creek–Reese Creek, Bear Creek, Rescue Creek–Rattlesnake Butte, Deckard Flat, and Crevice Creek. Turner (1955) suspected that rattlesnakes may be found farther downstream from the Reese Creek area and farther upstream from the Crevice Creek area. He even mentioned a possible report of them in the Hellroaring Creek area near Tower Junction (Skinner 1926 *cited in* Turner 1955).

Abundance/Status

We have observed prairie rattlesnakes to be locally common. However, even in Yellowstone National Park, rattlesnakes have suffered persecution at the hands of humans. In the 1930s and 1940s, Rudolph Grimm submitted annual reports documenting the number of rattlesnakes killed by him and his staff each year. In 1938, Grimm reported to the park superintendent: "32 rattlers killed this year." Of course, at that time Grimm was simply doing what he believed was right, and what was probably his job, just as government trappers had killed the last wolves in the region a decade previously. At the Stephens Creek site, we found the remains of a wooden and wire mesh snake trap at the main entry/exit point of the rattlesnake den. This trap may even have been the very same trap used by Grimm 55 years ago to catch and kill snakes.

Fortunately, people have slowly gained a greater appreciation for all animals, predators and prey alike, and we now are learning to accept that a rattlesnake or a wolf is not "good" or "bad," just as elk and deer should not be given a value based on human biases and emotions.

In the interviews conducted by Aubrey Haines (see above sec-

Unfortunately, like wolves and other predators, rattlesnakes were persecuted up through at least the 1930s in Yellowstone. A former Park Service employee provided annual reports to the Superintendent of the number of rattlesnakes killed at this Stephens Creek den site. This old wood and wire trap at the mouth of the den was likely used to catch and kill these snakes. Today, rattlesnakes are well protected in the park, and we have observed many individuals of a variety of age classes here and elsewhere. Notice the ground here and in the background of the photograph is rocky and the vegetation is sparse. This is representative of areas that are very hot and dry, which is typical of rattlesnake habitat in Yellowstone.

tion on distribution), men who drove stagecoaches in Yellowstone in the early 1900s concluded that rattlesnakes were less abundant along the Gardiner-to-Mammoth road in 1961 than they were earlier this century. It is likely that in the heavily used travel corridor between Gardiner and Mammoth, humans removed enough rattlesnakes over an extended period of time to have long-term effects on their occurrence and abundance here.

Even today, some Yellowstone rattlesnake populations may only be partially protected. Even though the National Park Service now strives to protect *all* animal species, be they predator or prey, one rattlesnake den from which animals may migrate to and from Yellowstone Park actually lies outside park boundaries. We have never visited the Bear Creek den site, but learned of its existence from a Gardiner, Montana, resident, who told of visiting the den site in the springtime and killing rattlesnakes. This person was simply acting in a manner commonly accepted by his peers. Although a few people do eat rattlesnakes and their hides are sometimes used for decorative clothing, many people kill rattlesnakes simply for the sake of killing them or because they fear them. In our opinion, fear or ignorance are not justification for killing rattlesnakes.

Natural History
HABITAT.   Prairie rattlesnakes overwinter communally in the northern part of their range. These den sites are usually located in talus on south-facing slopes (Klauber 1972). In central Wyoming, rattlesnakes may disperse along straight paths away from the den for up to 10 km (6 mi), apparently stopping when they find a high concentration of rodents on which to prey (Duvall et al. 1990). Pregnant rattlesnakes generally remain within a kilometer (0.6 mi) of the den site and often aggregate in "rookery" areas, possibly because of the availability of warmer microclimates (Duvall et al. 1985). Rattlesnakes are well adapted to warm, arid conditions. The area where prairie rattlesnakes occur in Yellowstone receives only about 30 cm (12 in.) of precipitation each year, most of which falls in winter, and temperatures regularly exceed 32°C (90°F) in the summertime. It is the warmest, driest part of both Yellowstone and Grand Teton National Parks. The vegetation primarily consists of sagebrush and grasslands.

ACTIVITY PATTERNS.   In Yellowstone National Park, prairie rattlesnakes probably emerge from hibernation during April or May and presumably remain in the vicinity of the den for several weeks before dispersing. We have observed as many as 18 adult prairie rattlesnakes and one juvenile at the Stephens Creek den site in mid-May in Yellowstone. We have two other reports of rattlesnakes active near this den site in late April. According to studies of this species elsewhere in its range, these snakes probably spend most of the summer foraging for food. Pregnant females may do little else but maintain near constant body temperatures through most of the summer so that their embryos can develop and be born before the weather turns cold. In the northern part of their range, prairie rattlesnake males begin searching for mates in mid- to late summer. Breeding usually occurs away from the den (Duvall et al. 1985), and females usually do not breed more often than every other year in northern latitudes, and perhaps even less frequently. By late October, most, if not all, of the rattlesnakes probably will have returned to the den site and will have entered hibernation. We have a report of a prairie rattlesnake observed near the Yellowstone River in September 1941, one day after a snowfall.

During the spring and fall, most rattlesnake activity is probably restricted to the daytime. In the summer, rattlesnakes probably are most active in the morning and evening, especially on warm days (Gannon and Secoy 1985). Baxter and Stone (1985) report that rattlesnake foraging at night in Wyoming may be limited because of the cool nighttime temperatures of the region.

Like many reptiles, female rattlesnakes are adept at behaviorally maintaining relatively high (30°C, 86°F), relatively constant, body temperatures when they are pregnant (Vince Cobb, Idaho State University, personal communication, 1994), shedding, or digesting a meal and when environmental conditions are not limiting.

Rattlesnakes may live many years, especially in areas like Yellowstone where the active season is limited due to the region's long, cold winters. For instance, timber rattlesnakes (*Crotalus horridus*) in New York can live up to 25 years (Brown 1993). Like the spotted frog, rattlesnakes found in Yellowstone may be able to live several times longer than rattlesnakes in a southern desert climate where individuals may be active for much of the year.

The number of rattles on an individual snake does not necessarily tell the age of a rattlesnake. Rattlesnakes gain a new rattle each time they shed their skin. If a rattlesnake still has the "button" (the original knob on the end of the tail with which it was born), you may be able to tell how many times the average rattlesnake in the region sheds its skin in a given year. However, the number of times rattlesnakes shed their skin may range from zero to two or more times a year, depending on how fast they grow. Furthermore, the distal segments of the rattle may break off at any time. Ectothermic animals in seasonal climates can be aged relatively accurately by examining growth rings in certain bones, similar to counting growth rings of a tree.

FEEDING HABITS.   Prairie rattlesnakes prey on lizards, birds, and small mammals such as young rabbits, gophers, prairie dogs, mice, voles, and ground squirrels (Klauber 1972). Brown (1950 *cited in* Turner 1955) reported that a rattlesnake killed a small rabbit near the Stephens Creek nursery.

The prairie rattlesnake's loreal pits, located between the snout and the eye, sense longwave, infrared (heat) radiation. This unique organ is sensitive and accurate enough to allow the prairie rattlesnake to successfully strike at an animal with a warm body temperature in complete darkness, if the need exists. Of course, the tongue (which is used to "smell" via the Jacobson's organ on the roof of the mouth) and the eyes usually help the rattlesnake locate the prey.

Rattlesnakes are generally "sit-and-wait" predators. Unless they are moving to a new location or are searching for a mate, they are not readily encountered crawling about. They probably spend most of their time during their active season coiled under a sagebrush or rock or in a burrow, waiting for a small mammal to pass by.

A prairie rattlesnake's fangs are hollow and very sharp. When the snake strikes, venom flows through the fangs and into the puncture wounds created by the fangs. Small prey items are usually quickly immobilized and then eaten. The fangs eventually will be shed and replaced by new fangs.

Rattlesnakes can gain most of their water from the food they eat, either directly from the water content of the prey or by metabolizing the prey to produce water molecules. Rattlesnakes also drink water. A Great Basin rattlesnake in an outdoor enclosure was twice observed to drink rainwater that appeared to have been purposefully trapped in its coils (Aird and Aird 1990).

ENEMIES/DEFENSE.   Many species of birds and mammals are known to kill prairie rattlesnakes, including hawks, eagles, badgers, coyotes, deer, and pronghorn. The birds of prey and carnivores eat the snakes whereas the deer and pronghorn apparently kill rattlesnakes to protect themselves or their young (Klauber 1972). It's also possible that during hibernation or on cool nights, rodents may "turn the table" on rattlesnakes and kill or partially eat individuals slowed by cool temperatures.

Probably the most effective technique that rattlesnakes employ to avoid predators is simply to try to remain undetected. Many times, rattlesnakes do not rattle and simply go unnoticed. They blend in well with their surroundings and have relatively low levels of activity. They usually are close to a rocky crevice or burrow into which they can readily flee. However, if an animal ventures too close to a rattlesnake, the snake will usually make its presence known by rattling. This behavior does not mean a strike will inevitably follow; it just means that the snake "wants" you to avoid it. One theory concerning the evolution of the rattle is that it allowed snakes to warn animals such as bison so the snakes would not be stepped on (Klauber 1972). Vibrating the tail when threatened is a common behavior in many species of snakes, both harmless and venomous.

If they cannot escape, prairie rattlesnakes can defend themselves by striking and injecting venom, but they usually are reluctant to do so. In our experience with this rattlesnake species, we have been impressed with their attempts to avoid humans. During our observations of rattlesnakes at dens in Yellowstone, we never were struck at, even when we moved the snakes with snake hooks. Some rattlesnakes will actually hide their heads under their coils rather than strike (Duvall et al. 1990, Vincent Cobb, Idaho State University, personal communication, 1992). In the Pacific Northwest from 1950 to 1959, more people died of bee or wasp stings than rattlesnake bites (10 deaths from stings and only 1 from a snake bite) (Nussbaum et al. 1983). Even though most prairie rattlesnakes try hard to avoid contact with predators and humans, they are capable of inflicting a serious bite. They therefore should be treated with caution and respect. Most poisonous snake bites in this country are the result of people trying to handle or kill snakes.

In Yellowstone there are only two known cases of people being bitten by rattlesnakes (Lee Whittlesey, Yellowstone National Park Historical Archivist, personal communication, 1994). In 1945,

John French, a trail crew laborer, was bitten and recovered quickly. And in 1886, "Red River Dick" was bitten. Only the snake died from the event. As was reported in the July 10, 1886, edition of the *Livingston Enterprise:* "Speculation is now rife as to which received the most poison from the kiss, the snake or Dick. It is the general opinion that there was a mutual exchange, as there is no proof that the snake was killed from any other cause."

REPRODUCTION/DEVELOPMENT. Unlike most other species of snakes, prairie rattlesnakes in the northern part of their range breed in mid- to late summer, when the males cease foraging and begin searching for mates (Duvall et al. 1985; Dr. David Duvall, University of Wyoming, personal communication, 1988). Ritualized combat may occur between males to determine which males will have the opportunity to breed (Klauber 1972). This combat usually involves two males approaching and rising up against each other, attempting to gain leverage with which to "throw down" their opponent. A male may court and copulate with a female over a period of many hours. The sperm is apparently stored in the reproductive tract of the female until the following spring when ovulation occurs. After fertilization, pregnant females usually seek out warm microenvironments (especially in piles of suitably sized rocks) near the den site and spend most of the summer in gestation. Many females may aggregate in the same area, even under the same rock (Duvall et al. 1990). They may not eat at all during this gestation period.

From 4 to 21 live young are born in late summer; they may average 23 cm (9 in.) in length (Turner 1955). The mothers may remain with the young until after they shed their skins for the first time (within about 10 days) (Duvall et al. 1985; Dr. David Duvall, personal communication, 1988; Vincent Cobb, personal communication, 1992). Because of the short active season for these snakes in the Yellowstone region, females probably are on a biennial or longer reproductive schedule; that is, they cannot reproduce every year. It also probably takes several years for the young to reach sexual maturity. Female timber rattlesnakes in New York reach sexual maturity in 7 to 11 years (Brown 1991).

Other Reported or Potential Species

WE KNOW OF FOUR other species of amphibians and reptiles that either have been reported or that may occur in Yellowstone or the Tetons, but for a number of reasons the occurrence of persistent populations has not yet been either confirmed or rigorously discounted. Keep in mind that Yellowstone Park was more than a century old before the valley garter snake was first collected within its borders, and the northern sagebrush lizard was not confirmed to exist in the Tetons until 1992. Will another vertebrate animal species be confirmed in either national park? We think this question is one of the more interesting challenges facing professional and amateur naturalists in Yellowstone or the Tetons, and we encourage the reader's assistance. Use the species described in this section as a starting point to explore. Remember that collecting anything from either national park is illegal without a special permit.

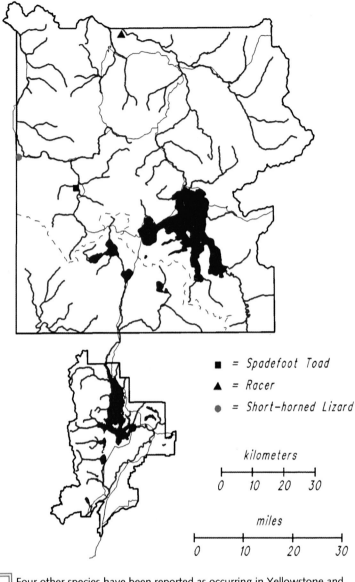

■ = *Spadefoot Toad*

▲ = *Racer*

● = *Short-horned Lizard*

kilometers

0   10   20   30

miles

0   10   20   30

Four other species have been reported as occurring in Yellowstone and Grand Teton National Parks. Racers have been reported along the lower Yellowstone River near Gardiner, Montana. Short-horned lizards have been reported from along the Madison and Firehole Rivers, and spadefoots have been reported from along the Firehole River. Painted turtles have been reported recently near Old Faithful and Yellowstone Lake, but were probably released pets. However, one historic collection record exists for painted turtles, as well as one each for short-horned lizards and spadefoots, but not for racers. Whether populations of any or all of these species have occurred, or still do occur in the region remains open to question.

152

Spadefoot
Spea intermontana or *bombifrons*

Spadefoots have been reported twice from Yellowstone Park—once in a museum collection from before the turn of the century. Spadefoots look like other toads, including the boreal toad, except spadefoots have a shorter snout with relatively larger eyes and less warty skin. We have searched only briefly for this animal along Sentinel Creek near the Lower Geyser Basin along the Firehole River. Spadefoots usually occur in warmer climates in the western United States. Therefore, we predict that if they were to occur in this region, they may be dependent on a geothermal heat source for survival. We suspect that if spadefoots occur here, they would be the plains spadefoot, rather than the Great Basin spadefoot. Look for spadefoots in dry habitats with seasonally flooded wetlands.

The two species of spadefoots that could occur in the region covered by this book are either the Great Basin spadefoot (*Spea intermontana*) or the plains spadefoot (*Spea bombifrons*). Some herpetologists use the generic name *Scaphiopus* instead of *Spea*. These animals are often called spadefoot toads. Although toadlike, they are not really true toads (family Bufonidae), but are members of the family Pelobatidae.

Great Basin and plains spadefoot toads are quite similar but can be distinguished from each other by comparing the condition of the bumps between their eyes and the "spades" on their hind feet. They reach a length of about 60 mm (2.4 in.), with the females slightly larger than the males. Their heads are short with blunt snouts. Their pupils are vertically elliptical (like a cat). Both species have a rounded bump (called a boss) between the eyes. The boss of Great Basin spadefoots is soft and glandular, whereas the boss of plains spadefoots is harder because it is underlain by bone. The eardrum (tympanum) is relatively small. The innermost toes on the front feet of breeding males have nuptial pads. The hind feet are webbed. Both species have a single, dark tubercle or "spade" on each of their hind feet. This tubercle is relatively long and narrow in the Great Basin spadefoot and relatively short and broad in the plains spadefoot (Baxter and Stone 1985). The ground color of these spadefoots is gray, brown, or green with dark mottling. The darkness of individuals varies with temperature and light (Baxter and Stone 1985) and also is correlated with the color of the substrate (Nussbaum et al. 1983). Light dorsolateral stripes may be present and may form an hourglass pattern. Great Basin spadefoots usually have a dark, brown spot on the upper eyelids (Stebbins 1985). The ventral surface is light colored. The skin is relatively smooth.

The only species that you would likely confuse with a spadefoot in our area is the boreal toad. Boreal toads differ from spadefoots in having horizontal pupils; two tubercles on each hind foot; a rougher, wartier skin; and large parotoid glands.

Spadefoots are known to occur in the area around Yellowstone and Grand Teton National Parks (Stebbins 1985). Plains spadefoots occur to the east and north of Yellowstone, east of the continental divide. Great Basin spadefoots occur to the east, south, and west of Grand Teton National Park, mostly west of the continental divide.

We know of only two reports of spadefoots from the parks. Turner (1955) cited Cope (1889) stating that a spadefoot was recorded from "Camp Thorne, Yellowstone." Turner speculated that this site could have been well outside park boundaries, and in view of the ecological requirements of this species he would not expect to find spadefoots in the park.

We also have a record of a spadefoot observed in the Sentinel Creek drainage (a tributary to the Firehole River), just less than 1 km (0.5 mi) downstream of Fairy Falls. On a clear morning in June 1982 at 10:30 a.m., John Cancalosi saw what he believed to be a spadefoot in this area. We have been unable to spend much time in the field following up on this observation.

Spadefoots can be difficult to find unless the conditions are appropriate (for example, rainy nights in the spring or summer). It would be most unusual to find spadefoots seemingly so far removed from other known populations at lower elevations. However, the area in which Cancalosi's observation was made is geothermally influenced. Recall that the sagebrush lizard persists in geothermally heated areas in Yellowstone far removed from, and at higher elevations than, other known lizard populations.

Of the two species of spadefoots found around the parks, we speculate that in this part of Yellowstone the plains spadefoot would be more likely to occur than the Great Basin spadefoot. The basis for this speculation is that the Firehole River drainage (the location of Cancalosi's observation) is east of the continental divide and a tributary of the Madison River. Plains spadefoots are known to occur at lower elevations along this river.

Western Painted Turtle
Chrysemys picta belli

Painted turtles are the only species of turtle ever reported from the region. If painted turtles occur here, they could not be confused with any other amphibian or reptile known to occur in Yellowstone or the Tetons. They have been reported several different times, but we suspect that most of these reports are released pets (an illegal act in the parks). However, scientists on the Hayden Expedition in 1871 reported collecting a turtle from the shores of Yellowstone Lake. Why turtles would then seem to be absent there today remains a mystery to us. Look for painted turtles near shallow wetlands with emergent vegetation.

The only species of turtle that might occur in Yellowstone or the Tetons is the western painted turtle, a member of the water and box turtle family (Emydidae). It is a medium-sized turtle, reaching a shell length of up to 240 mm (9.5 in.) in Wyoming (Baxter and Stone 1985). Males are smaller than females. The shell is relatively flat and smooth. The dorsal surface of the shell is dark green or black, and the ventral surface is reddish orange with a dark, central marking extending to the edge of the shell. Yellow stripes occur on the head and limbs. Males have longer front claws than females.

The painted turtle ranges over most of the eastern United States and the Great Plains and extends into the Pacific Northwest. Isolated populations are found in Colorado and New Mexico (Stebbins 1985). This species is known to occur east and north of Yellowstone National Park. In Wyoming, painted turtles are found only in eastern counties below about 1850 m (6000 ft) (Baxter and Stone 1985). Thompson (1982) reported that the painted turtle has been collected within the Greater Yellowstone Ecosystem to the north of the park in Montana.

Several records exist concerning the possible occurrence of painted turtles within our area. One of the first explorers of the Yellowstone country, F. V. Hayden, reported collecting a painted turtle in the region. Lee Whittlesey (Yellowstone Park Historical Archivist, personal communication, 1994) clarified for us that, on page 486 of Hayden's Fifth Annual Report of his 1871 trip, Dr. E. D. Cope reported a specimen of *"Chrysemys oregonensis"* collected at "The Yellowstone Lake." Yeager (1929) commented on the painted turtle as follows: "Although by no means common in the Yellowstone, this turtle is occasionally found in the ponds and marshes. It is a variety of the common painted or pond turtle found so extensively throughout the country." He then continued, quoting the description found in Hurter's *Herpetology of Missouri* (1911).

We know of no solid evidence that a population of turtles was ever found in Yellowstone. We are aware of only scattered, single observations at high-elevation areas like Bridge Bay on Yellowstone Lake and Isa Lake at Craig Pass. These recent individual sightings occurred only within one summer season, and according to the descriptions they were probably released pets that did not survive.

We are also unaware of any reports of turtles being found in the Tetons. There have been no reliable observations of turtles adjacent to or within the border of Yellowstone Park on the Yellowstone River or along the Snake River in the Tetons — both likely distribution routes for turtles to enter Yellowstone or the Tetons. Also, there have been no confirmed reports of wild turtles anywhere else in either park in the last 124 years, despite the fact that these animals tend to be very visible where they are known to occur. Therefore, like Turner (1951, 1955), we conclude that presently there are probably no native turtles in Yellowstone or the Tetons. We have no good explanation for the turtle reported by Cope in the 1871 Hayden expedition.

Eastern Short-horned Lizard

Phrynosoma douglassii brevirostre

Short-horned lizards are readily distinguishable from sagebrush lizards (the only other lizard species known to occur here) by their "collar" of short, rounded horns that project posteriorly, and by their round, flattened body shape. They have been reported occurring in the Madison River drainage, including one collection record over a century old from along the Firehole River. Also, some have speculated that this lizard species would be more likely to occur in the Tetons than the sagebrush lizard, which was only recently confirmed in that park. Look for short-horned lizards in dry, sunny, rocky areas, or areas with some geothermal influence.

159

Eastern short-horned lizards are members of the family Phrynosomatidae. In Wyoming, they can reach a length of about 7 cm (2.8 in.) (Baxter and Stone 1985). Their bodies are rounded and flattened, with a fringe consisting of a single row of soft spines separating the dorsal and ventral surfaces (Stebbins 1985). Short, rounded horns project posteriorly from the rear edge of the head. The legs and tail are relatively short. The ground color is brown or gray. There are brown blotches on the back and often speckles of white. The belly also is white. The back of the body is covered with small, granular scales interspersed with keeled scales; the belly scales are flat and platelike (Baxter and Stone 1985). The rounded shape and horns of this species easily distinguish it from the sagebrush lizard.

This species ranges from extreme southern Canada to Mexico and from the crest of the Cascades east to Montana, Wyoming, Colorado, and New Mexico. Its range nearly encircles Yellowstone and the Tetons. In Wyoming, its range encompasses the whole state below 2000 m (6500 ft) (Baxter and Stone 1985). This species has been collected within 25 km (15 mi) of the south boundary of Grand Teton National Park in the Snake River drainage (Baxter and Stone 1985). Thompson (1982) reported this species as occurring in the Greater Yellowstone Ecosystem north of the park in Montana. Linder (1989) stated that his interpretation of the distributional literature indicated this species would only be found in suitable habitat at the periphery of the Greater Yellowstone Ecosystem, reasonably far from either park boundary. Nevertheless, a collection record over a century old exists in the U.S. National Museum for this species from the Firehole River basin. Turner (1955) wrote: "This lizard was originally reported from the Upper Firehole Basin. . . . One might be tempted to view this old record with some skepticism but for the fact that on June 14, 1954, Merrill Beal collected a juvenal [sic] horned lizard near the West Entrance checking station. The extent and size of the population remains unknown at present." Turner (personal communication, 1989) validated the reliability of Merrill Beal's observation near the West Entrance to Yellowstone.

One might think that if this species were to exist in Yellowstone, it would likely occur in the lower Yellowstone River area upstream of Gardiner, Montana, and the collection made by Beal may have been a released pet. Turner (personal communication, 1989) says both he and Beal suspected this to be the case.

According to the collection record from the Smithsonian Museum, this species apparently occurred in Yellowstone historically. Also, as with the spadefoot, the heavily geothermally influenced Firehole River basin would be the most likely area to harbor a relict population of horned lizards. However, the occurrence of a population of short-horned lizards in Yellowstone remains questionable.

It is also possible that short-horned lizards could occur in the Tetons; they can be difficult to find and may simply have escaped detection. Remember that short-horned lizards have been collected just 25 km (15 mi) south of the park boundary. Also recall that the sagebrush lizard was not confirmed in the Tetons until 1992. Indeed, upon reviewing a draft version of this book, Dr. George Baxter (personal communication, 1993) stated: "From my experience with the distribution of lizards in the state [of Wyoming], I would not have been surprised to find the horned lizard more common in the Jackson Hole valley than the [northern] sagebrush lizard."

Eastern Yellow-Belly Racer
Coluber constrictor flaviventris

The eastern yellow-belly racer is often found in the same habitats as the rattlesnake and bull snake, and a well-documented observation was indeed reported from along the lower Yellowstone River in just such habitat near Gardiner, Montana. However, this remains the only observation, and the only mention, of this species for either park. These racers are readily distinguishable from most snake species known to occur in the region by their uniform green-gray color. They are more slender than rubber boas, and have larger eyes and move much more quickly. Juvenile racers can often look like a bull snake or rattlesnake, but racers have smooth scales compared to these other two species.

The eastern yellow-belly racer is a member of the family Colubridae, the largest family of snakes. It is a slender, medium-sized snake, reaching a total length of up to 113.5 cm (45 in.) in Wyoming (Baxter and Stone 1985). It has prominent eyes and smooth scales. In adults, the dorsal color is uniformly bluish or grayish green, the belly is yellow, and the throat is white. The dorsal coloration of the juveniles is different than that of the adults; it consists of many brown blotches and spots on a pale background.

Because of their smooth scales and uniform dorsal coloration, adult racers might be confused with rubber boas. However, racers are slimmer, have larger eyes, are usually lighter colored, and are much quicker than rubber boas. Juvenile racers are sometimes confused with either bullsnakes or even rattlesnakes. The smooth scales of the racer distinguish it from both of these species.

Racers range over most of the United States except for the desert southwest. Their confirmed range approaches Yellowstone most closely in the north (Stebbins 1985). In Wyoming, racers are found in most of the counties east of the continental divide, below about 2150 m (7000 ft) (Baxter and Stone 1985). Thompson (1982) reported that the racer has been collected in the Greater Yellowstone Ecosystem north of the park in Montana, in the Yellowstone River drainage.

During our initial search for herpetological distribution data, we found in the park files a convincing report of an eastern yellow-belly racer about 5.6 km (3.5 mi) upstream from Gardiner, Montana, into the park on the Yellowstone River trail. Park naturalist Joe Zarki and a friend made the observation in April 1984. Although we believe their description is thorough and reliable (especially after conducting a personal interview with Zarki), it remains the only observation of this species within park boundaries. Unfortunately, although Zarki archived a photograph of the snake somewhere in the files at Yellowstone's headquarters, we have been unable to relocate the photograph. Even Yeager (1929) and Turner (1951, 1955) fail to mention the possibility of this species being found in Yellowstone. However, the chance that the one observed specimen was introduced by a person into the area where it was observed seems remote to us.

Because racers can frequently be found in the same habitat as rattlesnakes and bullsnakes and because we found the latter two species when searching the area from which the racer was reported, it is plausible to believe that racers could exist in this part of the park. Two possible explanations for the presence of the racer in Yellowstone are: (1) either the one observation of a racer in the park was truly anomalous and the racer is not found in Yellowstone, or (2) racers are present in Yellowstone but they have escaped detection over the last 120 years or, more likely, they have been observed on other occasions but never reported. We have spent some time in the area where the observation was made, but we have not had the opportunity to repeatedly search for racers there. Assistance from the reader is needed here. We also have a report of a racer on the upper Gardner River upstream from Swan Lake Flats near Indian Creek Campground on the Mammoth-to-Norris road.

Racers also may occur in the Gallatin River drainage in the northwest portion of Yellowstone Park. Two collection records are reported for this species just west of Yellowstone, apparently along the Gallatin River itself, within 1–2 km (0.5–1 mi) from the park boundary (Davis and Weeks 1963).

We also found museum records of racers collected approximately 30 km (18 mi) downstream from Grand Teton National Park, south of Hoback Junction in Hoback Canyon. Because they are west of the continental divide, these records are probably for western yellowbelly racers (subspecies *C. c. mormon*).

Information Needs
How You Can Contribute

IT SHOULD BE clear by now that although much is known about the amphibians and reptiles of Yellowstone and Grand Teton National Parks, even more remains to be learned about specific life-history features and specific distribution limits of these animals within the two parks. It should also be clear that you can definitely contribute meaningfully to our collective knowledge, as many people already have (see, for example, the sagebrush lizard distribution account). All it takes is careful, thoughtful observation coupled with equally meticulous documentation and, most importantly, sharing of that knowledge by submitting your observations to park headquarters so they can be included in park files. Photographs of the animals and of their general habitat are very helpful. Also remember that the activity of these animals depends greatly on temperature, so measurements of water and air temperature with a thermometer are useful. Finally, carry this book with you to help with your observations: Use the observation form provided at the end of this section or, better yet, obtain an observation form from the national parks themselves.

Addresses for submitting your observations are:

Yellowstone National Park, Resource Management Office
P.O. Box 180
Mammoth, WY 82190

Grand Teton National Park, Resource Management Office
P.O. Box 170
Moose, WY 83012

For future research in Yellowstone and Grand Teton National Parks, we will obtain these records from the parks. However, if you wish to report observations directly to us or if you have questions you need answered, you may contact us:

Dr. Charles R. Peterson
Department of Biological Sciences
Idaho State University
Campus Box 8007
Pocatello, ID 83209
(208) 236-3922

The best way to identify where information is needed is to look at the preceding section on other reported or potential species and at each species account. New and original observations can be made for all species and in many areas of both parks. However, the need for information about some species and some regions of the parks (for example, backcountry areas) are particularly outstanding.

If you suspect that you have observed a species that is not listed in the table of contents of this book, it is crucial to provide an accurate description of the animal with its exact location; a photograph of both the animal and the general area would be valuable. Take at least two photos: one for you and one for the National Park Service files.

We think that the racer, spadefoot, and eastern short-horned lizard are currently the three best candidates for being documented as new species for either national park.

As far as we can tell, the northern leopard frog does not now occur in either national park, although it once occurred in the Tetons and adjacent to Yellowstone (see species account). Even though it is listed in the table of contents, we would consider a new observation of this species in the Tetons to be important in light of its disappearance here and in light of serious declines in its abundance elsewhere in its range (see section on declining amphibian populations in the introduction). Again, observations must be carefully documented, and photographs of the animal and the general area would help greatly.

The northern sagebrush lizard was only confirmed as existing in the Tetons in 1992, and we have received other observations of it in new areas in both the Tetons and in Yellowstone (see species account). Its occurrence in these new areas must be documented, either with multiple observations at various times from different people or with good photographs of both the animal and the general area in which it is observed. New and important insights may be gained about the distribution and life history requirements of the northern sagebrush lizard in the Greater Yellowstone Ecosystem with new observations of this species in areas where its existence has yet to be confirmed (for example, along the Snake River in Grand Teton National Park).

The distribution of the valley garter snake in both national parks is far from completely understood (see species account). Keep in mind that in addition to the Snake and Falls River drainages, this species may also occur in the Gardner and Yellowstone River drainages in the north near Gardiner, Montana.

The only species for which we have excellent life history information based on data collected within the Greater Yellowstone Ecosystem is the spotted frog. A fair amount is also known about the northern sagebrush lizard here. But even for these species, the data were collected in one general area, and many other regions of both parks remain to be explored. Spotted frog and northern sagebrush lizard activity in the Tetons or in northern Yellowstone may be quite different from that documented in the center of Yellowstone. For most other species, we are unsure about even the most basic things, such as when amphibians lay their eggs in different portions of the region, or when those eggs hatch, or when reptiles emerge from hibernation and breed. Also, what do these animals eat and what eats them?

Finally, remember that we know very little about the distribution of all these species in backcountry areas (areas away from roads). Look at the distribution maps for each species and read the written accounts of their distributions. If you make an observation of which you are certain in an area for which no dot occurs on the distribution map, report it. If you plan to spend time in the backcountry and you have a desire to make and submit careful observations of amphibians and reptiles, you can almost count on providing new, useful information.

Amphibian and Reptile Observation Form

Please provide whatever information you can, even if you are unsure of the species.

Species: _____ Number of Animals _____

Observation Date: _____/ _____/ _____ Time: _____ AM PM (circle one)

Observer Name(s) _____ Phone No.: _____

Affiliation: _____

Address:_____

Have you seen this species before? _____

Description of Animal (size, color, pattern, pupil shape, skin texture, etc.):
_____ photo? _____

Description of Animal's Behavior: _____

_____

Animal's Location: (Be as accurate as possible; e.g., 4.5 miles north and 3.3 miles east of known landmark; Latitude and Longitude; UTM coordinates; **or** Range, Township, and Section):

_____

_____

County _____ State _____

Habitat: _____

_____

Weather: (temperature, cloud cover, wind, etc.):

_____

Remarks: _____

Please return to:
  Dr. Chuck Peterson
  Idaho Museum of Natural History
  Box 8007, Idaho State University
  Pocatello, Idaho 83209
  (208) 236-3922 office   236-4570 FAX

Instructions for Filling Out the Amphibian and Reptile Observation Form

Please provide whatever information you can.

Common Name/Species: Provide the common or scientific name of the animal if you are able to identify it. If you cannot identify it, please describe it as accurately as possible. Include the exact or estimated number (1–10, 10–100, more than 100, etc.) observed.

Date: Include the year and clearly distinguish between day and month (for example, 6 June 1992).

Time. Include AM or PM or use the 24-hour time system.

Please include your name, affiliation, address, and **phone number** so we can contact you if we need further information, a copy of the photograph, and so on.

Have you seen this species before?

Description: Describe the animal as accurately as you can so we can confirm your identification or so we can identify it from your description. Characteristics to note include size/length, shape, color, pattern (for example, striped, banded, blotched, or unicolor), skin texture (for example, smooth, shiny, rough, scaled, etc.), pupil shape (round or elliptical), and presence or absence of limbs and tail. See the references below for more information on identifying characteristics. Did you photograph the animal?

Behavior: Behavioral descriptions are useful in identifying animals and are inherently interesting. For example: Was the animal moving or still? Did it crawl or jump or hop? Was it fast or slow? Was it trying to escape from you or was it hunting or feeding? Did it vocalize? What did it sound like?

Location: Be as accurate as possible. Try to describe the site so that someone else could relocate it from your directions. For example, in a small pond, 30 yards north of Highway X, 4.5 miles N and 3.3. miles E of a known landmark (junction, the center of a town, etc.). Please include the exact coordinates if you know them (latitude and longitude, UTMs, or range, township, section, quarter section, etc.). Accurate locality information can greatly enhance the value of your observation.

Habitat: Describe the major environmental features (such as forested mountainside, valley meadow, river, lake, etc.) and the immediate area around the animal (burrow, talus slope, streambank, etc.).

Weather: Include such information as the air temperature, water temperature, wind conditions, cloud cover, precipitation, etc.

Remarks: Please include any other information you consider relevant.

Useful References

Baxter, G. T., and M. D. Stone. 1985. Amphibians and reptiles of Wyoming. 2d ed. Cheyenne: Wyoming Game and Fish Dept. 137 pp.

Leonard, W. P., H. A. Brown, L. C. Jones, K. R. McAllister, and R. M. Storm. 1993. Amphibians of Washington and Oregon. Seattle: Seattle Audubon Society. (Excellent color photographs)

Nussbaum, R. A., E. D. Brodie, and R. M. Storm. 1983. Amphibians and reptiles of the Pacific Northwest. Moscow: University of Idaho Press. 332 pp. (The best general source of information on the amphibians and reptiles of Idaho)

Stebbins, R. C. 1985. A field guide to western reptiles and amphibians. Boston: Houghton Mifflin Co. 336 pp. (The best field guide to the amphibians and reptiles of the western United States)

Glossary

Amphibian Members of a class of animals with smooth, moist skin, gelatinous eggs, and a two-phase life cycle in which the animals metamorphose from a larval to an adult form.

Amplexus Clasping of a female by a male frog or salamander during mating.

Anuran Member of an order of amphibians that lack tails, that is, the frogs and toads.

Axolotl Ancient Aztec name for the larval form of the tiger salamander.

Caudal Pertaining to the tail; for example, the caudal scales of reptiles are those on the ventral surface of the tail.

Cloaca The single chamber through which the contents of the digestive, excretory, and reproductive systems pass. Opens to the outside at the vent (cloacal opening).

Crepuscular Primarily active during low-light periods of morning and evening.

Diurnal Active during the day.

Dorsolateral folds Glandular ridges along the sides of the back of some frogs.

Ectotherm An animal whose body heat is derived primarily from the environment (for example, solar radiation); a cold-blooded animal.

Endotherm An animal whose body heat is derived primarily from metabolic activity; a warm-blooded animal.

Genus A category in the classification of plants and animals that is between the species level and the family level. For example, both garter snake species in this book belong to the same genus but belong to a different family than rattlesnakes or rubber boas. The classification of the wandering garter snake, in descending order, is as follows:

> Class Reptilia (reptiles)
>> Order Squamata (lizards and snakes)
>>> Family Colubridae (common snakes)
>>>> Genus *Thamnophis*
>>>>> "Species" *elegans*
>>>>>> Subspecies *vagrans*

Geothermal Describing a source of heat within the ground (volcanic activity) that is responsible for hot springs and geysers.

Gravid   Describing a female amphibian or reptile carrying ripe eggs or embryos.

Habitat   Specific place where a plant or animal lives.

Herpetofauna   Amphibian and reptile species within a given area.

Herpetology   The study of amphibians and reptiles.

Intercostal grooves   Vertical grooves along the sides of some salamanders.

Labial scales   Scales along the upper and lower lips of snakes and lizards.

Larva   Immature form of amphibians, between the egg and adult stages (for example, frog tadpoles or larval tiger salamanders [axolotls])

Loreal pits   Infrared heat sensing organs on the face of "pit" vipers (for example, the prairie rattlesnake) that help locate and strike at prey items.

Metamorphosis   Transition from a larval form (for example, larval salamander or tadpole) to an adult form (for example, salamander or frog).

Neoteny   For amphibians, the condition of prolonged larval period or failure to metamorphose at the normal time. Often intended to include attainment of sexual maturity in the larval form.

Nocturnal   Active during the night.

Paedogenesis   The precocious development of sexual maturity in larval individuals (for example, larval salamanders).

Reptile   Members of a class of animals with dry scaly skin and direct development (no larval form) and that breathe through lungs; includes turtles, crocodilians, tuataras, snakes, and lizards.

Species   A category in classification of plants and animals between the subspecies and the genus level. For example, the two gopher snake subspecies potentially included in this book are of the same species, but are of a different genus than all the other amphibians and reptiles here. (See **Genus**)

Subspecies   The most restrictive formal category in the classification of plants and animals. It is less inclusive than that of all other levels of classification, with the exception of informal categorizations such as "race" or "population." (See **Genus**)

Tadpole   Larval frog or toad.

Thermoregulation   Control of body temperature within a relatively narrow range, primarily accomplished behaviorally by ectothermic animals.

Toe Pads   Enlarged discs on the end of the toes of members of the tree frog family.

Vent   Cloacal opening.

References Cited

Agerter, K. S. 1932. A record snake found. Yellowstone Nature Notes 9(6–7):33.

Aird, S. D., and M. E. Aird. 1990. Rain-collecting behavior in a Great Basin rattlesnake (*Crotalus viridis lutosus*). Bull. Chicago Herpetol. Soc. 25(12):217.

Albertson, H. 1928. A new genus for Yellowstone. Yellowstone Nature Notes 5(9):6–7.

Algard, G. A. 1968. Distribution, temperature and population studies of *Sceloporus graciosus* in Yellowstone National Park. M.S. thesis, Montana State University, Bozeman.

Baxter, G. T., and M. D. Stone. 1985. Amphibians and reptiles of Wyoming. 2d ed. Cheyenne: Wyoming Game and Fish Dept. 137 pp.

Bellairs, A. d'A., and S. V. Bryant. 1985. Autonomy and regeneration in reptiles. Pp. 301–410 *in* Biology of the Reptilia, vol. 15. Edited by C. Gans and F. Billett. New York: Wiley. 731 pp.

Black, J. A. 1970. Amphibians of Montana. No. 1 of Animals of Montana Series. Montana Wildlife, Jan. 1970:1–32.

Black, J. H., and R. B. Brunson. 1971. Breeding behavior of the boreal toad, *Bufo boreas boreas* (Baird and Girard), in western Montana. Great Basin Nat. 31(2):109–113.

Blaustein, A. R., P. D. Hoffman, D. G. Hokit, J. M. Kiesecker, S. C. Walls, and J. B. Hayes. 1994. UV repair and resistance to solar UV-B in amphibian eggs: A link to population declines? Proc. Nat. Acad. Sci. 91:1791–1795.

Borell, A. E. 1931. Note on the food habits of a rubber snake. Copeia 3:131.

Bragg, A. N. 1965. Gnomes of the night: The spadefoot toads. Philadelphia: University of Pennsylvania Press. 127 pp.

Brodie, E. D. III. 1990. Genetics of the garter's getaway. Nat. Hist. 7:45–50.

Brown, W. S. 1991. Female reproductive ecology in a northern population of the timber rattlesnake, *Crotalus horridus*. Herpetologica 47:101–115.

———. 1993. Biology, status, and management of the timber rattlesnake (*Crotalus horridus*): A guide for conservation. Soc. Study Amphibians and Reptiles Herpetol. Circ. No. 22. 78 pp.

Bryan, T. S. 1986. The geysers of Yellowstone. Boulder, CO.: Associated University Press. 299 pp.

Campbell, J. B. 1970. Food habits of the boreal toad, *Bufo boreas boreas*, in the Colorado Front Range. J. Herpetol. 4(1):83–85.

Carpenter, C. C. 1953a. An ecological survey of the herpetofauna of the Grand Teton–Jackson Hole area of Wyoming. Copeia 1953 (3):170–174.

———. 1953b. Aggregation behavior of tadpoles of *Rana p. pretiosa*. Herpetologica 9:77–78.

———. 1954. A study of amphibian movement in Jackson Hole Wildlife Park. Copeia 1954 (3):197–200.

———. 1955. Aposematic behavior in the salamander *Ambystoma tigrinum melanostictum*. Copeia 1955(4):311.

Charland, M. B. 1991. Reproductive ecology of female garter snakes (*Thamnophis*) in southeastern British Columbia. Ph.D. dissertation, University of Victoria, Victoria, B.C. 206 pp.

Clark, T. W. 1981. Ecology of Jackson Hole, Wyoming: A primer. Salt Lake City: Paragon Press. 110 pp.

Collins, J. T. 1990. Standard common and current scientific names for North American amphibians and reptiles. 3d ed. Soc. Study Amphibians and Reptiles Herpetol. Circ. No. 19.

Cooper, W. A., C. P. Ohmart, and D. H. Dahlsten. 1978. Predation by a rubber boa on chestnut-backed chickadees in an artificial nesting site. Western Birds 9:41–42.

Cope, E. D. 1889. The Batrachia of North America. Bull. U. S. Nat. Mus. No. 34:1–525.

Corn, P. S. 1993. Life history notes: Anura. *Bufo boreas* (boreal toad). Predation. Herpetol. Rev. 24(2):57.

Corn, P. S., and R. B. Bury. 1990. Sampling methods for terrestrial amphibians and reptiles. Gen. Tech. Rep. PNW-GTR-256. Portland, OR: U.S. Dept. Agric., Forest Service, Pacific Northwest Res. Sta. 34 pp.

Corn, P. S., and J. C. Fogelman. 1984. Extinction of montane populations of the northern leopard frog (*Rana pipiens*) in Colorado. J. Herpetol. 18:147–152.

Corn, P. S., and L. J. Livo. 1989. Leopard frog and wood frog reproduction in Colorado and Wyoming. Northwest. Nat. 70:1–9.

Corn, P. S., W. Stolzenburg, and R. B. Bury. 1989. Acid precipitation studies in Colorado and Wyoming: Interim report of surveys of montane amphibians and water chemistry. Biol. Rep. 80(40.26). Air Pollution and Acid Rain Report No. 26. 57 pp.

Davis, C. V., and S. E. Weeks. 1963. Montana snakes. Helena: Montana Dept. of Fish and Game. 10 pp.

DeLacy, W. W. 1876. A trip up the south Snake River in 1863. Contrib. Hist. Soc. Montana 1:130–132. Helena, MT: Rocky Mountain Publishing Co.

Devine, M. C. 1975. Copulatory plugs in snakes: Enforced chastity. Science 187(4179):844–845.

———. 1977. Copulatory plugs, restricted mating opportunities and reproductive competition among male garter snakes. Nature 267(5609):345–346.

Duellman, W. E., and L. Trueb. 1986. Biology of amphibians. New York: McGraw-Hill Book Co. 669 pp.

Duvall, D., M. B. King, and K. J. Gutzwiller. 1985. Behavioral ecology and ethology of the prairie rattlesnake. Nat. Geogr. Res. 1(1):80–111.

Duvall, D., M. J. Goode, W. K. Hayes, J. K. Leonardt, and D. Brown. 1990. Prairie rattlesnake vernal migrations: Field experimental analyses and survival value. Nat. Geogr. Res. 6:457–469.

Erwin, D. B. 1974. Taxonomic status of the southern rubber boa, *Charina bottae umbratica*. Copeia 4:996–997.

Gannon, V. P. J., and D. M. Secoy. 1985. Seasonal and daily activity patterns in a Canadian population of the prairie rattlesnake, *Crotalus viridis*. Can. J. Zool. 63:86–91.

Grothe, S. 1992. Red-tail hawk predation on snakes: The effects of weather and snake activity. M.S. thesis, Idaho State University, Pocatello. 103 pp.

Hayes, M. P., and M. R. Jennings. 1986. Decline of ranid frog species in western North America: Are bullfrogs (*Rana catesbeiana*) responsible? J. Herpetol. 20(4):490–509.

Heath, A. G. 1975. Behavioral thermoregulation in high altitude tiger salamanders, *Ambystoma tigrinum*. Herpetologica 31:84–93.

Hildebrand, M. 1974. Analysis of vertebrate structure. New York: John Wiley and Sons. 710 pp.

Hill, S. R. 1995. Description of migratory chronology of adult tiger salamanders (*Ambystoma tigrinum*) and survey of larvae of the tiger salamander in the northern range of Yellowstone National Park. Master's thesis, Montana State University, Bozeman, Montana.

Hill, S. R., and R. E. Moore. 1994. Herpetological survey in the northern range of Yellowstone National Park. Ann. Rept. Yellowstone National Park. February 1, 1994. 21 pp.

Hoyer, R. F. 1974. Description of a rubber boa (*Charina bottae*) population from western Oregon. Herpetologica 30(3):275–283.

Hurter, J. 1911. Herpetology of Missouri. Trans. St. Louis Acad. Sci. 20:59–274.

Jacobson, A. 1926. Snakes come out of hibernation. Yellowstone Nature Notes 3(5):5

Keiter, R. B., and M. S. Boyce (eds.). 1991. The Greater Yellowstone Ecosystem: redefining America's wilderness heritage. New Haven: Yale University Press.

Kiester, A. R. 1971. Species density of North American amphibians and reptiles. Syst. Zool. 20:127–137.

Klauber, L. M. 1972. Rattlesnakes: Their habits, life histories, and influences on mankind. 2d ed. Berkeley: University of California Press. 1536 pp.

Knight, D. H., and L. L. Wallace. 1989. The Yellowstone fires: Issues in landscape ecology. BioScience 39(10):700–706.

Koch, E. D., and C. R. Peterson. 1989. A preliminary survey of the distribution of amphibians and reptiles of Yellowstone National Park. Pp. 47–49 *in* Rare, sensitive and threatened species of the Greater Yellowstone Ecosystem. Edited by T. W. Clark, D. H. Harvey, R. D. Dorn, D. C. Genter, and C. Groves. Jackson, Wyoming: Northern Rockies Conservation Cooperative, with Montana Natural Heritage Program, The Nature Conservancy, and Mountain West Environmental Services.

Leonard, W. P., H. A. Brown, L. L. C. Jones K. R. McAllister, and R. M. Storm, 1993. Amphibians of Washington and Oregon. Seattle, Wash.: Seattle Audubon Society.

Licht, L. E. 1975. Comparative life-history features of the western spotted frog, *Rana pretiosa*, from low- and high-elevation populations. Can. J. Zool. 53(9):1254–1257.

Linder, A. D. 1989. Short-horned lizard. Pp. 50–51 *in* Rare, sensitive and threatened species of the Greater Yellowstone Ecosystem. Edited by T. W. Clark, D. H. Harvey, R. D. Dorn, D. C. Genter, and C. Groves. Jackson, Wyoming: Northern Rockies Conservation Cooperative, with Montana Natural Heritage Program, The Nature Conservancy, and Mountain West Environmental Services.

Linder, A. D., and E. Fichter. 1977. The amphibians and reptiles of Idaho. Pocatello: Idaho State University Press. 78 pp.

Miller, R. R., and C. L. Hubbs. 1960. The spiny-rayed cyprinid fishes (*Plagopterini*) of the Colorado River system. Misc. Publ. Mus. Zool. Univ. Michigan, No. 115.

Mueller, C. F. 1967. Temperature and energy characteristics of the sagebrush lizard in Yellowstone National Park. Ph.D. dissertation, Montana State University, Bozeman. 38 pp.

———. 1969. Temperature and energy characteristics of the sagebrush lizard in Yellowstone National Park. Copeia 1969 (1):153–160.

Mueller, C. F., and R. E. Moore. 1969. Growth of the sagebrush lizard, *Sceloporus graciosus*, in Yellowstone National Park. Herpetologica 25(1):35–38.

Nussbaum, R. A., E. D. Brodie, and R. M. Storm. 1983. Amphibians and reptiles of the Pacific Northwest. Moscow: University of Idaho Press. 332 pp.

Parker, W. S., and W. S. Brown. 1980. Comparative ecology of two colubrid snakes, *Masticophis t. taeniatus* and *Pituophis melanoleucus deserticola* in northern Utah. Milwaukee Public Museum, Publ. Biol. Geol. No. 7. 104 pp.

Patla, D. A., and C. R. Peterson. 1994. The effects of habitat modification on a spotted frog population in Yellowstone National Park. Final report to the University of Wyoming/National Park Service Research Center. Cheyenne: University of Wyoming. 11 pp.

Peterson, C. R. 1987. Daily variation in the body temperatures of free-ranging garter snakes. Ecology 68:160–169.

Peterson, C. R., A. R. Gibson, and M. E. Dorcas. 1993. Snake thermal ecology: The causes and consequences of body temperature variation. Pp. 241–314 *in* Snakes: Ecology and behavior. Edited by R. A. Seigel and J. T. Collins. New York: McGraw-Hill Publishing Co.

Peterson, C. R., E. D. Koch, and P. S. Corn. 1992. Monitoring amphibian populations in Yellowstone and Grand Teton National Parks. Final report to the University of Wyoming/ National Park Service Research Center. Cheyenne: University of Wyoming. 25 pp.

Phillips, K. 1990. Where have all the frogs and toads gone? Bioscience 40(6):422–424.

Pierce, S. 1987. The lakes of Yellowstone. Seattle: The Mountaineers, 306 Second Ave. West, Seattle, WA 98119.

Platz, J. E. 1989. Speciation within the chorus frog (*Pseudacris triseriata*): Morphometric and mating call analyses of the boreal and western subspecies. Copeia 1989(3):704–712.

Porter, W. P., and C. R. Tracy. 1983. Biophysical analysis of energetics, time-space utilization, and distributional limits. Pp. 55–83 *in* Lizard ecology: Studies of a model organism. Edited by R. Huey, E. Pianka, and T. Schoener. Cambridge: Harvard University Press.

Romme, W. H., and D. G. Despain. 1989. Historical perspective on the Yellowstone fires of 1988. BioScience 39(10):695–699.

Schullery, P. 1989. The fires and fire policy. BioScience 39(10): 686–694.

Skinner, M. P. 1926. The Yellowstone nature book. Chicago: A. C. McClurg Co. 221 pp.

Stebbins, R. C. 1985. Western reptiles and amphibians. The Peterson Field Guide Series. Boston: Houghton Mifflin Co. 336 pp.

Taigen, T. L., and K. D. Wells. 1985. Energetics of vocalization by an anuran amphibian (*Hyla versicolor*). J. Comp. Physiol. B155: 163–170.

Tanner, V. M. 1931. A synoptical study of Utah amphibia. Contrib. Dept. Zool. Entomol., Brigham Young Univ. No. 40. 198 pp.

Thompson, L. S. 1982. Distribution of Montana amphibians, reptiles, and mammals. Bozeman: Montana Audubon Council. 24 pp. (L. S. Thompson, 101 Pine St., Helena, MT 59601)

Thorson, T., and A. Svihla. 1943. Correlation of the habitats of amphibians with their ability to survive the loss of body water. Ecology 24:374–381.

Tinkle, D. W., A. E. Dunham, and J. D. Congdon. 1993. Life history and demographic variation in the lizard *Sceloporus graciosus*: A long term study. Ecology 74(8):2413–2429.

Turner, F. B. 1951. A checklist of the reptiles and amphibians of Yellowstone National Park with incidental notes. Yellowstone Nature Notes 25(3):25–29.

———. 1952. Peculiar aggregation of toadlets in Alum Creek. Yellowstone Nature Notes 26(5):57–58.

———. 1955. Reptiles and amphibians of Yellowstone National Park. Yellowstone Interpretive Series No. 5. Mammoth, WY: Yellowstone Library and Museum Association. 40 pp.

———. 1958a. Life history of the western spotted frog in Yellowstone National Park. Herpetologica 14:96–100.

———. 1958b. Some parasites of the western spotted frog, *Rana p. pretiosa*, in Yellowstone National Park, Wyoming. J. Parasitol. 44(2):182.

———. 1959. An analysis of the feeding habits of *Rana p. pretiosa* in Yellowstone National Park, Wyoming. Am. Midl. Nat. 61(2): 403–413.

———. 1960. Population structure and dynamics of the western spotted frog, *Rana p. pretiosa* Baird and Girard, in Yellowstone Park, Wyoming. Ecol. Monogr. 30(3):251–278.

Varley, J. D., and P. Schullery. 1983. Freshwater wilderness: Yellowstone fishes and their world. Mammoth, WY: Yellowstone Library and Museum Assoc. 132 pp.

Webb, R. G., and W. L. Rouche. 1971. Life history aspects of the tiger salamander, *Ambystoma tigrinum mavortium*, in the Chihuahuan desert. Great Basin Nat. 31:193–212.

Williams, J. E., and D. W. Sada. 1985. Status of two endangered fishes, *Cyprinodon nevadensis mionectes* and *Rhinichthys osculus nevadensis*, from two springs in Ash Meadows, Nevada. Southwest. Nat. 30:475–484.

Woodward, B., and S. Mitchell. 1992. Temperature variation and species interactions in aquatic systems in Grand Teton National Park. Pp. 140–145 *in* University of Wyoming/National Park Service Research Center, 16th Ann. Rept.

Worthing, P. 1993. Endangered and threatened wildlife and plants: Finding on petition to list the spotted frog. Federal Register Notice, U.S. Dept. Interior, Fish and Wildl. Serv., 50 CFR Part 17. Friday, May 7, 1993. 58(87):27260–27263.

Wuerthner, G. 1991. Yellowstone: A visitor's companion. Harrisburg, PA: Stackpole Books. 218 pp.

Yeager, D. C. 1926. Miscellaneous notes. Yellowstone Nature Notes 3(4):7.

———. 1929. Reptiles of Yellowstone Park with notes on the Amphibia. Yellowstone Nature Notes. Mammoth, WY: Yellowstone National Park Library.

Additional References

This section includes literature that is not cited in the text.

Aller, A. R. 1951. Hydrophily in *Charina*. Herpetologica 7:84.

Bauman, J. S. 1950. Migration of salamanders. Yellowstone Nature Notes 24(1):4.

Black, J. A. 1970. Turtles of Montana. No. 2 of Animals of Montana Series. Montana Wildlife, Nov. 1970:26–32.

Breitenbach, R. P. 1951. Large fish for a small snake. Yellowstone Nature Notes 25(6):70.

Brown, E. 1950. Rattlesnake kills rabbit. Yellowstone Nature Notes 24(4):47.

Carpenter, C. C. 1953. Trapping technique for aquatic salamanders. Herpetologica 8:183.

Cutter, R. 1930. Ike and Mike. Yellowstone Nature Notes 12(7):12.

Elmore, F. 1954. Gopher snake vs. ground squirrel. Yellowstone Nature Notes 28(3):35.

Lystrup, H. T. 1952. A garter snake captures a young bird. Yellowstone Nature Notes 26(1):10.

Pierson, M. A. 1950. Mysterious Mr. salamander. Yellowstone Nature Notes 24(2):23.

Pope, P. H. 1931. A new record for the rubber snake. Yellowstone Nature Notes 13(9):70.

Reinhard, E. G. 1930. Another snake note. Yellowstone Nature Notes 8(9):70.

Turner, F. B. 1952. Duel in the sun. Yellowstone Nature Notes 26(5):59.

————. 1953. New localities for the northwestern tiger salamander (*Ambystoma tigrinum melanostictum*) in Yellowstone Park. Yellowstone Nature Notes 27(5):58.

————. 1953. Rattlesnake near Stephens Creek. Yellowstone Nature Notes 27(6):72.

Watson, W. V. 1951. Rattlesnake. Yellowstone Nature Notes 25(4):47.

About the Authors

Edward "Ted" Koch and Charles R. "Chuck" Peterson met at Idaho State University in the fall of 1988 and began what has turned into a productive and pleasant, personal and professional relationship. Ted was a candidate for a master of science degree and Chuck was a newly arrived assistant professor in the Department of Biological Sciences at Idaho State University.

The work presented in this book started as a simple herpetology class project. The original goal was to examine the distribution and abundance of amphibians and reptiles in Yellowstone National Park, based on existing information. When Ted told Yellowstone's chief of research John Varley about this project during a routine update on the status of his fish research in the park, John immediately responded with enthusiasm and encouraged Ted and Chuck to continue to pursue it. It is this kind of support and encouragement from a wide range of people that made this book possible.

Ted received his bachelor's degree in environmental biology from Southern Connecticut State University in 1985 and then studied fish ecology at Idaho State University, from which he graduated with a master of science degree in zoology in 1990. His master's research project was on the trout of the Firehole River in Yellowstone Park. Previously he had worked in Yellowstone in 1985 with the U.S. Fish and Wildlife Service and presently works for this agency in Boise, Idaho. He has always had an interest in amphibians and reptiles since he grew up catching frogs and snakes in his back yard in Connecticut. He has also had an interest in and periodically conducted research on or worked with birds and mammals.

Chuck is an associate professor of ecology and physiology in the Department of Biological Sciences at Idaho State University and curator of herpetology at the Idaho Museum of Natural History. He received his bachelor's degree in 1972 and master's degree in 1974 from the University of Illinois in Urbana. He earned his

Ted Koch (left) and Chuck Peterson, during one of their many sampling trips, at Little Slide Lake near Mannoth, Wyoming in the northern portion of Yellowstone Park (photograph by Roy Wood).

Ph.D. from Washington State University in 1982. He then conducted five years of postdoctoral work at the University of Chicago. In the fall of 1988, he joined the faculty at Idaho State University. His research interests are in physiological and behavioral ecology, biogeography, and conservation biology of amphibians and reptiles.

Index

Aggregation, of tadpoles and toads, 56, 57

Algard, George, 9, 10, 100, 103

Altitudinal limits, of amphibians, 28; of reptiles, 93

Alum Creek, 57

Ambystoma tigrinum melanostictum, species account, 30–44

Amphibians, definiton of, 27–29

Amplexus, 46, 54, 70, 79

Askey, Chris, 19

Axolotls, 29, 42

Backcountry, 2, 11, 110, 166, 167

Bar BC Ranch, 99

Bartelt, Paul, xii, xviii, 50, 52

Baxter, George, 118, 135, 161

Beal, Merrill, 160, 161

Bear Creek, 96, 120, 143, 144

Beaupre, Steve, 89

Bechler region, 85, 110, 128

Biodiversity, importance of in protecting amphibians and reptiles, 17

Biomass, 16

Biscuit Basin, 76

Blacktail Butte, 116

Blacktail Patrol Cabin, 116

Blotched tiger salamander, species account, 30–44

Boiling River, 116, 120, 141

Boreal chorus frog, species account, 58–68

Boreal toad, species account, 45–57

Boundary Creek, 98

Bufo boreas boreas, species account, 45–57

Bullfrog, species account, 88–90

Bullsnake, species account, 114–22

Calling frogs, 29. *See also* boreal chorus frog; boreal toad; spotted frog

Camp Thorne, Yellowstone, 155

Cancalosi, John, 155

Carpenter, Charles, contributions of, 7–10

Carroll College, 110

Central Michigan University, 129

Charina bottae, species account, 106–13

Chorus frog. *See* boreal chorus frog

Chrysemys picta belli, species occurrence, 156–58

Clark, Ray, 52

Cloaca, 42, 107, 137, 167

Cobb, Vince, 122, 146, 148

Cole, Glen, 98

Colter Bay, 36, 37, 99

Coluber constrictor flaviventris, species occurrence, 162–64

Coluber constrictor mormon, 164

Common garter snake. *See* valley garter snake

Common names, use of, xv

Conservation biology of amphibians and reptiles, declines in abundance, 17, 19–22

Continental divide, significance of in the region, 6, 12

Cope, E. D., 157, 158

Crevice Creek, 116, 143

Crotalus horridus, 146

Crotalus viridis viridis, species account, 139–49

Data sources, 10, 11

Death Canyon, 48, 110

Deckard Flat, 143

Decline, of amphibian populations, 9, 19–22; of boreal toad in the region, 48; of northern leopard frog in the region, 87

Description of region, 1–7

Dorcas, Mike, xii, 110, 111

Drought, 21, 28, 50, 82

McClure, Craig, 19
McGill University, 70
Madison River, 52, 84, 155
Mammoth Hot Springs, 37, 98, 116, 119, 128, 144
Mary Lake, 98
Metamorphosis, 29, 56, 82
Migration, in tiger salamanders, 37–40
Mimicry, in bull snakes, of rattle-snakes, 121
Missouri River, 6, 85
Monitoring of amphibian populations, 9, 21, 22
Montana State University, xii, 9, 35, 41, 95, 100, 103, 129
Moore, Robert, 95
Mount Washburn, 98
Mueller, Charles, contributions of, 9
Museum collection record, xviii

National Park Service, xi, 9, 98, 144, 165, 166
Norris Geyser Basin, 98, 100–103
Northern leopard frog, species account, 83–87
Northern sagebrush lizard, species account, 94–105

Observations, how to document, 10, 165–70
Old Faithful, 7, 76, 98, 112, 128

Paedogenesis/paedomorphism, 42
Painted turtle. See western painted turtle
Phelps Lake, 98
Photographs, necessity of, 165–69
Phrynosoma douglassii brevirostre, species occurrence, 159–61
Physical environment of the region, 1
Pilgrim Creek, 98–100
Pituophis catenifer deserticola, species occurrence, 118
Pituophis catenifer sayi, species account, 114–22
Population size, 16; monitoring of, of amphibians, 9

Porcupine Hill, 98
Prairie rattlesnake, species account, 139–50
Pseudacris triseriata maculata, species account, 58–68

Racer, species occurrence, 162–64
Rana catesbeiana, species account, 88–90
Rana pipiens, species account, 83–87
Rana pretiosa, species account, 69–82
Rattlesnake. See prairie rattle snake
Rattlesnake Butte, 143
Ravens, predation of on toads, 53
Redpath Museum, 70
Red River Dick, 149
Red-sided garter snake, 134, 135
Reese Creek, 116, 143
Reptiles, definition of, 91–93
Rescue Creek, 143
Riparian habitat, importance of, 13, 15
Rocky Mountain National Park, 21, 87
Roughskin newt, 137
Rubber boa, species account, 106–13

Sagebrush habitat, importance of, 12–15
Sagebrush lizard. See northern sagebrush lizard
Scaphiopus, 154
Sceloporus graciosus graciosus, species account, 94–105
Scientific names, use of, xv
Seibert, Susan, 134
Shoshone Lake, 2, 38
Shoshone Lake Geyser Basin, 98
Signal Mountain, 37
Slide Lake, 35
Snake River, importance of to region, 2, 4
Southampton College, 19
Spadefoot, species occurrence, 153–55